Christine,

You are amazing!

I love your passion and zeal for the Lord and for the church.

God is going to continue using you in amazing ways!

Just keep being like him!

- Casey

© 2020 by Casey Noce

Published by Coffee House Publishing
www.coffeehousepublishing.com

Printed in The United States of America

Names: Noce, Casey
Title: Be Like Jesus
Description: Adrian, MI: Coffee House Publishing
[2020] | includes bibliographical references.
Identifiers: ISBN 978-1-7353284-1-6
Subjects: Religion/Spirituality

Illustrations by Alissa Reynolds

BE
LIKE
JESUS

ABOUT THE AUTHOR

Casey Noce is a pastor, coach, consultant, author, evangelist, camp fanatic, Survivor fan, and proud Michigander. He has dedicated his life to teaching people how to be like Jesus. 30 {Peace and Joy} was Casey's first published work. A simple 30 day devotional for "middle school men". Shortly after, Casey wrote Jesus Had A Beard, a book designed to help high school guys as they step into manhood with a Christ-like understanding of masculinity. Through the years, Casey has been involved in children's, youth, young adults, worship, and production ministries. He has served in big churches and small churches alike. Casey has spent the past seven years developing ministry curriculum and content for the churches he has served. He has also spent the same time coaching football, baseball, and yes, as you will read about in Chapter 13, soccer. Casey is the Director of Content at Coffee House Publishing. You can find Casey on Facebook and Instagram @caseynoce or online at caseynoce.com. He would love to connect with you and hear how you are doing in your journey to be like Jesus.

DEDICATION

To all those who taught me to Be Like Jesus.

My Family, you teach me how to be present.

Karis, you helped me live as a victor.

Pastor Neil, you showed me how to serve.

Art and James, you taught me how to share the Gospel.

Ben, you taught me to embrace the desert and love coffee.

CJ, you showed me what it looks like to lead like Jesus.

Pastor Chris, you taught me to sacrifice for the Gospel.

My Brothers, you remind me to stay humble.

Mom, you taught me about reciprocal submission.

Johnny Mac and Mark, you remind me to pursue my purpose.

Alissa, you helped me to create good whatever, wherever.

Steven, you showed me how to stay filled up in prayer.

Kyle, you taught me how to love and appreciate everyone.

Dad, you've always encouraged me.

My Students, you teach me every day to live out the Gospel.

ABOUT THE ARTIST

Alissa Reynolds is a designer, illustrator, creative director, aspiring muralist, coffee mug collector, antique store enthusiast and lover of new ideas. Alissa is the Director of Creativity at Coffee House Publishing. Her pursuit of the creative fields, the creative life, and our Creator has given way to fascinations with unique artistic mediums, new places and different avenues of ministry. Alissa is passionate about walking alongside and empowering others as they go after what God has created them to do. She would love to connect with you and hear your story or a dream God has placed on your heart. You can connect with Alissa and find more of her art on Instagram @alissareynolds9.

ENDORSEMENTS

"Be Like Jesus is a great reminder to us that being like Jesus is a daily process of choosing to think, act, and feel like Jesus. After all, he did give us the right to become children of God. Thanks, Casey for modeling what it looks like to be like Jesus."

Doug Clay,
General Superintendent, Assemblies of God

"Be Like Jesus is truly a book with insights and inspirations from a young minister wise beyond his years. Honest and funny encouragement for new and old Christ-followers alike. Casey reminds us, this journey we are on is always teaching us how beautiful life can be when we strive to Be Like Jesus."

Jenn Pasquale,
Pastor, International Christian Fellowship Rome

"Be Like Jesus is an amazing challenge to be like Jesus in every area of our lives, told through stories you can easily relate to and understand. This book shows us that it is an everyday process to be like Jesus when we open our eyes to the world around us and follow the Holy Spirit's leading."

Braley Fryer,
Next Generation Pastor, Victory Family Church

ENDORSEMENTS

"Jesus was and still is the most polarizing figure to ever walk the planet. To understand his impact on the world would take a lifetime. Be Like Jesus is a transformative guide that gives us fresh vision on how to reflect and emulate the life of Christ. One read will jumpstart your faith today."

Peter Reeves,
Next Gen Pastor, Mt Hope Church

"Casey's book "Be Like Jesus" is a great reminder to all of us about what our main purpose in life truly is…to be like Jesus. It's easy to get side tracked with the busyness of life and ministry, but this book challenges you to get your focus back on Jesus. Jesus wants us to be like him in all that we do and say. This is also a great book for new believers to help them in their walk with Jesus. It will challenge new believers to look at their lives and see if they are living the way Jesus would want them to live."

Rev. Mary Boyd,
National BGMC Coordinator, Assemblies of God

"This book, written in the same teaching style as Jesus, is an unpacking of the astonishing work of God toward us and how we can be astonishing examples of Jesus in our world today. Casey gives us insights into the narratives of God in his life and helps us understand that Jesus is the author and finisher of our faith. When I started reading this book, I couldn't put it down. Your story is God's story too."

John Maguire,
Executive Director, Free2Play

ENDORSEMENTS

"Being like Jesus at times seems really, really hard. As a follower of Jesus, a husband, father, pastor, and friend, it seems I have more stories of failing to be like Jesus than I do succeeding. Through stories of late-night pool, welcome signs, popsicles, the color blue, yellow, and green, and an empty gas tank, it reminded me I have more stories of being like Jesus. As a father of one of Casey's students, I will always be thankful that Casey lived like Jesus more often than not."

CJ Clymer,
Lead Pastor, Newlife Church

"What would it look like if we took Jesus' New Testament teachings and put them in the context of modern-day life? As a reflection of Jesus' own teaching methods, Be Like Jesus utilizes the power of storytelling to encourage others to be imitators of Christ. Balancing humor and conviction, Casey Noce's new book unfolds the overlooked subtleties of Christ's interactions and translates them into their twenty-first century meanings. But like any good story, the book doesn't stop there. We are invited to join in a life lived for Christ and a life like Christ – a life far better than anything this world has to offer."

Hutson Hohlbein,
Student, Taylor University

CONTENTS

INTRODUCTION

My office trash can is overflowing with paper basketballs titled Chapter One.

I get into a concept about a few chapters, and then I bail.

It's like I wasn't supposed to be writing it all along. I start and then stop. Start and then stop. It got tiring. I love to write, so not having a book project in front of me made me feel like I wasn't able to be productive. I thought, maybe I'd write about holiness, or living a Christian life. Then, I thought I should write about leadership or as I would put it *followship*. Maybe I should write about influence and being impactful where you are. Though I had a slew of really marketable and catchy titles, I had no substance. Nothing stuck. One evening as I was driving home, I had a moment of inspiration that took me back to the beginning of the year.

In January I wrote down a word. Just one word… nothing special.
I wrote one simple word to help me maintain a focus for the year.
I had prayed about what word I should choose. To be honest, I heard nothing… until I went to a friend for prayer. He and his wife prayed over me and he said,

"Casey, I hear God saying the word PURPOSE."

Now, I didn't know what that meant, but I trusted my friend's ability to hear from the Lord. Sometimes God gives the answer to your prayer to someone else. We are better together and we need each other. I grabbed my phone, opened a note, and typed "Purpose".

I started praying about what this word meant.

Ephesians 5:1 came to mind.

"Therefore be imitators of God, as beloved children." [1]

Ephesians 5:1 ESV

This verse is short and simple. I quickly connected the dots. My purpose is to be like Jesus. My purpose is to respond to life's many ups and downs as Jesus would and even did. I am destined to become like him. Honestly, I don't just believe this is my purpose. I believe *be like Jesus* is your purpose too.

I believe God has called all of us to follow Jesus' example. Jesus is the perfect role model. As we imitate him, we are in for a treat. There is no better way to live!

I invite you to walk with me through a journey of becoming more like Jesus.

This will require a lot of grace, and mercy, and love; not only for others, but also for yourself.

I felt compelled to write this encouragement to you because I believe sometimes the message of how to live a Christian life gets complicated. We make our lives about a list of what not to do. We try to avoid certain things. We hang out with certain people. We work certain jobs. I know everyone reading this book has a desire to live a "good life", whatever that means. You know what this book is about. The title is self-explanatory. You know that throughout this book you will be challenged, encouraged, stirred up, and equipped to live like Jesus lived, to talk like Jesus talked, to think like Jesus thought, to be like Jesus.

Whether you're a pastor, teacher, business leader, parent, artist, student, athlete, or maybe you're Jeff Probst. I have written this simple little book to encourage you to join me, and billions of others in this great big world to,

BE
LIKE
JESUS

CHICKEN POT PIE SURVIVOR

BE PRESENT WITH THOSE AROUND YOU

CHAPTER 1

BE PRESENT WITH THOSE AROUND YOU

Some people connect with God best in a church. Others retreat to the great outdoors. But my pew is often my driver's seat. I love to drive. It's therapeutic. I like being able to focus on the road and watch things pass by me through the window. I have also learned that doing something with my hands helps me focus more. Like playing drums on the steering wheel. While I sing along with country radio. Yes, I like country music.

Please don't stop reading.

Driving helps me calm down. I get to clear my head. When I clear my head of all my thoughts, occasionally I hear one of God's thoughts.

Sometimes we don't hear God because we are too loud, we need to be quiet and listen for the whisper of the Holy Spirit.

I started thinking about the last book I had started and how I just didn't feel like it was time to write it. It discouraged me that I was quitting yet another book. Maybe I needed to stop writing. Maybe I needed to take a break.

Then, a God thought entered my mind.

It reminded me of my word for the year.

Purpose.

I started thinking again about my new motto, be like Jesus.

Of course! This had to be the book I was supposed to write. I started thinking of how I could lay the idea out in a practical, yet challenging way. I started thinking of stories that I could tell, verses I could quote, and people I could reference.

I had the best idea for an opening chapter.

I knew what I would do.

When I feel the inspiration to write, I run to my computer and begin typing as fast as I can.

But there was a problem… by the time I got home, I would have only twenty minutes before my friends came over to watch the season finale of my favorite T.V. show, Survivor… And, I still had to find time to make dinner.

I had everything ready to make chicken pot pie. Just making dinner would take about a half an hour. There's no way I could make dinner and write the beginning of a new book.

While I was stressing over missing the inspiration wave and subsequently missing the window to begin this new book, the Holy Spirit whispered to me.

"Jesus would rather eat chicken pot pie and watch Survivor with his friends than be productive."

Would he?

I thought about it for a minute. There is no specific reference to survival based reality shows, or chicken pot pies in the Bible.

Here's the thing; Jesus didn't live in twenty-first century America.

Jesus He lived in his time. He lived in his town. He lived in his culture.
So, instead of trying to insert the scripture into our present-day lives,
we need to insert our lives into the scripture. We need to understand
the context!

The question became, what were the things Jesus valued?

People

Finding out what Jesus values in the first step in becoming like
Jesus. We don't just want to imitate Jesus and act like he acted.

We want our very character to be transformed into his likeness.

2 Corinthians 13:15 says, **"And we all, with unveiled faces, behold-
ing the glory of the Lord, are being transformed into the same
image from one degree of glory to another. For this comes from
the Lord who is the Spirit."** [1]

We need to allow the Holy Spirit to actually make us like Christ.
We aren't actors, doing our best impersonations of Jesus.
We are literally changing who we are to be more like him.

When I ask the question, what were the things Jesus valued,
I am compelled to search the scriptures to identify how Jesus lived.
He made many things concerning his character abundantly clear.
I read story after story where Jesus was found around his friends.

I have references to lead me to believe he was a carpenter by trade.
I also know that Jesus was well educated. Yet, the overwhelming ma-
jority of stories depict Jesus, not with a hammer in his hand, not with
a pencil tucked behind his ear, but with his friends nearby.

Jesus valued his friends. He loved spending time with them.

There is one particular story in John 21 where Jesus is on the beach making breakfast for his friends. Jesus clearly prioritized serving his friends a meal over being busy. He encouraged them to take a break from their productivity and enjoy breakfast on the beach.

I reasoned, given what I know about Jesus through the scriptures, he would certainly spend time with his friends over being busy.

So, I went home and made dinner for my friends and watched Survivor.

I put off writing the beginnings of this very book to do what I believed Jesus would do if he were in my shoes. Even after deciding that, I still planned how the very situation could be written about. I had to stop myself from writing the story in my head.

JESUS PRIORITIZED THINGS THAT SEEMED UNPRODUCTIVE; WHEN IN REALITY, HE KNEW EXACTLY WHAT INVESTMENT WOULD GAIN THE GREATEST DIVIDEND.

I was struggling with being present in the moment. I was struggling with being divinely unproductive.

There's a good term, divinely unproductive.

Jesus prioritized things that seemed unproductive; when in reality, he knew exactly what investment would gain the greatest dividend. Sometimes the most meaningful thing we can do is slow down.

* my Parents Stop and take time to talk

That night, God taught me a lesson about priorities.

For Jesus, people are the priorities. Jesus isn't concerned with the busyness of work. He couldn't care less about the productivity of your schedule.

Jesus values people more than productivity.

6

To Jesus, nothing is more important than people.

There is a story in Luke 10 about two sisters, Mary and Martha.

Jesus was traveling through a town when Martha approached him.

Martha invited Jesus into her home.

Jesus never turns down an invitation to spend time with someone.

Jesus obviously accepted her invitation and went with Martha to her home.

Jesus quickly began talking to the people in the house.

He shared stories, parables, and tales about his recent travels.

He talked to them about his Father.

He joked about his disciples who were with him.

He filled the room with joy and encouragement and laughter.

All the while, Mary, Martha's sister, was sitting at Jesus' feet intently listening to every word.

Martha got Mary's attention with the snap of her finger as she scolded Mary to come help her clean and prepare refreshments for the guests.

Mary ignored her sister's beckoning. Instead, she sat back against Jesus and clung back on to every word he spoke.

Eventually, Martha spoke up. "Jesus!" She muttered, "Will you please tell Mary to come help me in the kitchen? I am trying to get work done while she just sits there unproductively!"

The room went silent.

Everyone listened for Jesus to respond.

Would he agree with Martha and rebuke Mary?

Would he side with Mary and correct Martha?

Would he say something no one would have expected?
(He did that a lot.)

With all eyes on Jesus, and no one speaking, all you could hear (aside from the crickets) was the thundering frustration in Martha's soul. Jesus looked down to Mary and smiled. Likewise, he smiled at Martha. "Martha." Martha looked in Jesus's eyes. His soft smile told her everything she needed to learn before he said a word.

"Martha. You are so busy. You are so stressed, trying so hard to impress me. You think I want to be served, but I came to serve. You think I want to be offered something, but I came to offer something to you. If you would slow down, like your sister Mary, you would receive me. I didn't come to your house to eat or drink. I came here because you invited me. I came here to spend time with you. That's what matters most. Mary knows that."

The story ends there.

It doesn't say so in this chapter, but I believe Martha listened to Jesus with tears filling her eyes and ran to him after he finished speaking. I believe she repented of her busyness and worry. How could you not? How could you be face-to-face with gentle Jesus and not change? Jesus wrapped Martha in an enormous hug and welcomed her to the conversation as the food burnt in the oven.

The next account of Mary and Martha we have is in John 11. It is this story that leads me to believe Martha repented.

"Now when Jesus came, he found that Lazarus had already been in the tomb four days. Bethany was near Jerusalem, about two miles off, and many of the Jews had come to Martha and Mary to console them concerning their brother. So when Martha heard that Jesus was coming, she went and met him, but Mary remained seated in the house. Martha said to Jesus, "Lord, if you had been here, my brother would not have died. But even now I know that whatever you ask from God, God will give you." Jesus said to her, "Your brother will rise again." Martha said to him, "I know that he will rise again in the resurrection on the last day." Jesus said to her, "I am the resurrection and the life. Whoever believes in me, though he die, yet shall he live, and everyone who lives and believes in me shall never die. Do you believe this?" She said to him, "Yes, Lord; I believe that you are the Christ, the Son of God, who is coming into the world." [2]

John 11:17-27 ESV

Notice how Martha runs out to meet Jesus.

This time, she doesn't focus on cleaning the house or pouring him a drink.

She knows that meeting with Jesus is the most important thing.

yes! I need to do this more

Jesus comforts Martha and encourages her that Lazarus will live again.

We see Martha in both stories. But her character is drastically different in the second account than the first.

In the first account, she is well prepared for Jesus to come into her home. She is trying to keep up appearances. She doesn't really know who Jesus is. She is more focused on herself.

She wants to look good.

She wants to be notable.

She wants to impress.

@ me

In the second story, Martha runs to Jesus with tears in her eyes.

She is less concerned with having it all together and more concerned with Jesus. She confesses that he is the Messiah. She has a basic understanding of the afterlife. She seems to get the picture.

What changed?

She spent time with Jesus.

Her understanding changed as she spent time with Jesus.

Her heart changed as Jesus spent time with her.

This is what happens when we strive to be like Jesus. We prioritize spending time with him while we go about our day. We allow him to change us and make us more like him. Martha has a defining shift in her character because she was humble enough to learn to be like Jesus!

Jesus' interaction with Mary and Martha is special. It is not an unfamiliar story at all. We can all empathize with Martha. We've all gotten too busy for our own good. We've all rearranged our values to put productivity in the number one spot. But when we look at Jesus and the example he sets, we see that he puts the person in front of him at the top of the list.

Jesus values people more than productivity.

He'd take a messy living room, chicken pot pie, and Survivor over a clean house, and a book chapter any day of the week.

I found myself acting like Martha in Luke 10, trying to get all of my tasks accomplished before everyone arrived.

I hadn't worked at all that day, so I was eager to have some actual work to do.

Jesus would shut the laptop and spend time with those who came to fellowship with him. So, that's what I did.

I forgot about the book for a while.

I put away the laptop.

I silenced my desire to be productive.

I focused on the friends with me.

I laughed with them.

I talked with them.

I ate with them.

I watched Survivor with them.

I played card games with them.

I processed through struggles with them.

I sang with them...

All until about two in the morning.

✳ Late nights are inevitable when you decide to be like Jesus.

Especially when chicken pot pie and Survivor are involved.

COOKIES
CHRISTIANS
SOLZHENITSYN

LIVE LIKE YOU'RE WINNING

CHAPTER 2

LIVE LIKE YOU'RE WINNING

I love cookies.

Chocolate chip.

Snickerdoodle.

Peanut Butter.

Even Oatmeal Raisin!

They are quick, portable, and delicious. Cookies have been a staple in the dessert industry for years. I have yet to meet a person who doesn't love these little treats. Legend has it these little delicacies became popular in the early 1700s.

Obviously, I would like to take some time here to make an argument that cookies played a pivotal role in the American Revolution. It only makes sense. By that time, cookies had been around for a few decades. Picture it! George Washington sitting at his desk planning the Battle of Yorktown while crumbles of flaky, buttery goodness fell onto the map. Thomas Jefferson smudging chocolate chunks on the first draft of the Declaration of Independence. Alexander Hamilton and his friend John Lawrence sharing a plate of Sugar Cookies while dreaming about the future liberation of the nation! What other snack could inspire such courage and valor? None but the cookie!

Rabbit trail over.

Moving onto the real reason I brought up the subject of these delectable goodies!

The word cookie comes from a Dutch word, koekje.

Sounds like, "coke" and "yeah".

Koekje were essentially antique thermometers. Back in the day, a baker wouldn't have thermometers in their ovens, or an option to pre-heat the ovens to a certain temperature while baking cakes.

They used koekje instead.

They would pour a dab of cake batter onto a sheet and place it in the oven. When the cake batter would rise and turn golden brown, they would know the oven was up to temperature.

The word koekje means little cakes.

These little cakes had the same ingredients as the big cake (koek). But they were smaller, and more portable. These treats quickly started to catch on as independent dessert items. Soon, they made their way to America where we adapted the word Koekje to Cookie.

When I think of the history of the cookie, I am reminded of the words of Jesus spoken before the ascension in John 16:7. **"Nevertheless, I tell you the truth: it is to your advantage that I go away, for if I do not go away, the Helper will not come to you. But if I go, I will send him to you."** [1]

In this moment, Jesus was comforting his disciples who knew Jesus had to go be with the Father. He told them it is better that he goes than stay. How can that be? And why does this passage remind me of cookies? I'm getting there… Just hang with me a little longer.

Follow Jesus' logic for a minute.

Jesus knows that the Gospel needs to spread to the entire world.

In 1 Timothy 2:4, we find that Jesus wants **"all people to be saved and come to the knowledge of the truth."** [2] In Acts 1:8 Jesus said, **"But you will receive power when the Holy Spirit has come upon you, and you will be my witnesses in Jerusalem and in all Judea and Samaria, and to the end of the earth."** [3]

Jesus' plan to save the world starts with you and me.

God's divine strategy for this effort is to empower ordinary humans with the power of the Holy Spirit, so we can do what Jesus did.

Jesus was just one person. But, if Jesus would ascend to the Father and send the Holy Spirit to empower the believers left behind, we could reach the world exponentially quicker. Therefore, it is obviously better that Jesus go, and send the Holy Spirit.

The more Holy Spirit empowered little Jesus' running around, the better!

The Holy Spirit is the power source of Jesus' life. Nobody can live like Jesus without the Holy Spirit. The Fruit of the Spirit, the Gifts of the Spirit, and the Power of the Spirit are all traits of Christ. Jesus was the way he was because of the union he had with the Father and the Holy Spirit. That same Spirit that empowered Jesus to heal the sick, bring sight to the blind, make fish fill a net, multiply food, calm storms, and raise the dead is the same Spirit that lives in you and me! Just like a cookie or "little cake" is composed of the same ingredients. Everything that was *in Christ* is now *in us* through the Holy Spirit.

We are gifted a relationship with the Holy Spirit not so we can go on doing our own thing, but so we can manifest the same attributes and actions as Jesus. the Holy Spirit makes us "little Christs".

"And in Antioch the disciples were first called Christians." [4]

Acts 11:26 ESV

This word Christians (Christianos in Greek), means follower of Christ. Some researchers believe the word was originally used derogatorily for followers of Christ and could be translated to mean "little Christs".

We do this same thing all the time in identifying children. If a child is particularly daring, we may call them a little Evel Knievel. If they love playing baseball, you might call them a little Babe Ruth. If they regularly go on tangents about the founding fathers favorite cookies, you would call them a little Casey Noce.

You get my point.

The term Christian is meant to identify the followers of Jesus with, well... Jesus.

> **EVEN IN THE DEEPEST OF LIFE'S DESCENTS, FAITH NOT ONLY GROWS, BUT IS BORN.**

We know the Greek word for Christ, Christos means anointed one. I don't believe it would be too far of a stretch to say the word Christianos could mean "little anointed ones". Which is what we are. The fact of the matter is, without the Holy Spirit's anointing, we cannot be like Jesus. We must have the same anointing as Jesus in order to be like him.

In Luke 4:18, Jesus quotes the prophet Isaiah and says, **"The Spirit of the Lord is upon me, because he has anointed me to proclaim good news..."** [5]

Jesus was the Anointed One, anointed by the very Spirit of God! We get to be like him and be called "little Christs" or "little anointed ones".

In the first few years of the Christian Church, persecution was a major issue. The Church hadn't yet been popularized, and it was still considered a dangerous fringe movement. In many parts of the world that is still the case.

As we read through the Epistles we find encouragement after encouragement to endure persecution and keep the faith. Being called a little Christ was no casual matter; this likely meant that you would have a zero dollar bounty on your head. Because of this reality, Christians relied on the Holy Spirit's power to make it possible for them to be like Jesus even amid the most intense persecution.

Many Christians have been and are being persecuted for their faith. Many face trials and tribulations too horrible to even comprehend. For many, persecution has grown their faith. The persecuted don't back down but grow more resolute. Even in the deepest of life's descents, faith not only grows, but is born. As is the case for Aleksandr Solzhenitsyn, a Russian author who against all odds found God in the darkness.

Solzhenitsyn's story stands out to me because he has manifested an attribute of Christ that few have the opportunity to truly develop. I call this "Living Like You're Winning".

Solzhenitsyn fought in the Second World War for the Russians. He was arrested and thrown into a labor camp for eight years. While living in a proverbial Hell on Earth, he rethought his life.

He threw off his ideologies of communism and atheism and embraced Christianity. He understood a simple truth that few grasp; his enemies may imprison his body, but his soul belongs to the Lord.

Dr. Jordan Peterson writes of Solzhenitsyn, in his revolutionary book 12 Rules For Life.

"Alexander Solzhenitsyn had every reason to question the structure of existence when he was imprisoned in a Soviet labor camp, in the middle of the terrible twentieth century. He had served as a soldier on the ill-prepared Russian front lines in the face of a Nazi invasion. He had been arrested, beaten, and thrown into prison by his own people. Then he was struck by cancer. He could have become resentful and bitter. His life had been rendered miserable by both Stalin and Hitler, two of the worst tyrants in history. He lived in brutal conditions. Vast stretches of his precious time were stolen from him and squandered. He witnessed the pointless and degrading suffering and death of his friends and acquaintances. Then he contracted an extremely serious disease. Solzhenitsyn had cause to curse God. Job himself barely had it as hard. But the great writer, the profound, spirited defender of truth, did not allow his mind to turn toward vengeance and destruction. He opened his eyes, instead." [6]

(12 Rules For Life, pp. 154)

Solzhenitsyn authored many great literary works centered on his afflictions. After the war he continued to write, but his works were not published due to the dangerous political climate in Russia; until the sixties, when he sensed the world was ready for his work.

In 1970, he won the Nobel Prize for Literature. This propelled him to international stardom. He never let his success dictate his lifestyle, however. He led a humble and modest life, not compromising on his strict Christian convictions. He took the broken and tragic life he had and offered it as an offering to God. His works and legacy would have vanished with his body upon his death, had he not determined that he was an overcomer.

Solzhenitsyn understood that he was no victim. In his reflections on his imprisonment, he took an entirely different perspective. He looked at his life and his early years and came to the conclusion that he had contributed to his suffering. In his youth, he had joined and support-ed the Soviet Army and communism. He hadn't stood up for what was true during his fanatic adolescence. He had found himself on the wrong side of history. He understood that his error and sin had played a role in his predicament. He knew he was not an innocent man. He understood he had sinned and was in some tragic way a contributor to his own sufferings.

Solzhenitsyn was sentenced to a life in some of the worst living envi-ronments humans have ever had to endure and stricken with a deadly disease. How was he not a victim? As I look at Solzhenitsyn's life story, I find a man who though in his youth was a communist, spent the rest of his life combating the communist ideology that had caused so much pain and death in the twentieth century. He certainly felt first-hand the pain it caused.

He was a hero. He was no victim.

And though he may have considered himself not innocent, he cer-tainly wasn't deserving of all the pain he had endured. He not only survived his sufferings, he developed and grew as a result of them. He had a unique resilience which makes his story so inspiring. But how did he come out of his suffering so strong? What was his secret?

He overcame the prisons by embracing a victor's mindset.

He writes in his book, The Gulag Archipelago, "It is a good thing to *think* in prison, but it's not bad in a camp either... While they openly claim your labor and your body, to the point of exhaustion and even death, the camp keepers do not encroach at all on your thoughts. They do not try to screw down your brains and to fasten them in place.

And this results in a sensation of freedom of much greater magnitude than the freedom of one's feet to run along on the level." [7]

(The Gulag Archipelago, pp. 305-306)

That's not a quote you expect to hear from a man as familiar with suffering as Solzhenitsyn. He knew he was not a victim. He knew that though his aggressors may harm him physically, even to the point of death, he was in control of his mindset. His mindset was the same as Jesus. He knew his ultimate freedom was something that transcended his physical reality.

Both Solzhenitsyn and Jesus were subject to terrible sufferings brought on by the hands of an oppressive and corrupt political system.

Though they were both brutally tortured and oppressed, they never let a victim mentality settle in.

A quick Google search of the barbaric Roman torture method known as Crucifixion would evoke pity for anyone subjected to such an atrocity. Yet, Jesus doesn't ask us for our pity. Jesus rejects our victimized interpretation of his execution. In Luke 23:28 he shocked the people at the scene by telling the women weeping to stop crying.

Why?

Jesus knew that what he was about to do was more victorious than victimized.

Jesus was not about to allow our understanding of the cross become a recollection of pity and injustice. He knew what he was doing!

He was about to win the battle against death, once and for all!

22

The Cross is VICTORY!

The key to this victorious mindset is the resolve that no matter what man can do to oppose us, they can never take our soul. Our soul belongs to God alone.

As the well-known contemporary hymn puts it,

> "No scheme of Hell
> No will of man
> Could ever pluck me from his hand." [8]

Amen!

If we truly want to be little Jesus', we need to show the world what we are made of. Are we made of the same toughness and resilience of Christ himself?

Or, will we show the world that we would rather embrace a victimhood mentality?

When I look at inspirations like Solzhenitsyn I am encouraged all the more to never consider myself a victim. Psalm 118:6 says, **"The Lord is on my side; I will not fear. What can man do to me?"** [9]

This is the attitude of a victor.

This is the mentality of Jesus.

Our culture struggles with a victim mentality. It seems like we are competing to see who can be the ultimate victim.

Everyone wants to be the victim rather than the aggressor.

Given only those two options, I understand why!

But what if there was another option?

What if you could be a righteous victor?

We tend to think there are only two roles for people to fit into:

1) The poor, oppressed worker, mistreated by his tyrannical boss...

or

2) The rich, villainous titan of industry who exploits his workers for his own personal gain...

We rationalize our situations through this flawed paradigm all the time.

When your boss takes advantage of you and you feel unappreciated or underpaid, you take the role of the victim. When your professor grades your work lower than you want, you play the victim. We assign the person who we feel mistreated us the role of selfish, power-hungry, jerk-face. And we assign ourselves the role of the pitiful, helpless, victim. We need to stop.

This Neo-Marxist way of dividing people by class and power has only given us two choices.

Will we be powerful and evil or weak and noble?

Solzhenitsyn would certainly advocate against such classifications. He himself saw first hand the horrendous natural progression of such ideologies.

I believe he would argue for the existence of a third role.

This is the role that he and Jesus played in the drama of human history.

The role of the noble victor!

Evil is real. Mistakes are real. Pain is real. But Jesus is also very real! And he made a way to walk in victory over injustice, pain, evil, and sin!

WE ARE VICTORS IN CHRIST JESUS!

Jesus and Solzhenitsyn both were horribly mistreated yet, they considered their victory secured.

They knew the power of the Cross.

They knew that sin is defeated.

They lived in a reality in which their soul aligned with the finished work of the Cross rather than the failed work of the enemy.

Listen, I get it.

I know what it feels like to be hurt by someone. I know what it feels like to be betrayed. I know what it feels like to have someone take advantage of you. I get it. We all get it! All of us share in the brokenness of the world and the evil nature of those who inhabit it.

However, when I look at a man like Solzhenitsyn, I'm compelled to re-evaluate my sufferings. In twenty-first century America, our sufferings pale in comparison to what this man endured. Furthermore, I look at the life of Jesus leading up to his death on Calvary.

How can I, after being mistreated by man, look to the cross and see my sufferings as anything but insignificant?

How can I look at the blood-covered face of my Lord as he utters **"Father, forgive them..."** [10] and even for a moment consider holding on to unforgiveness?

How could I consider myself a victim?

If Jesus, in his unjust suffering on the Cross did not condemn his oppressors, but continued to forgive and offer salvation - how could I in my privileged environment, comfy bed, and fancy clothes even consider playing the role of a victim?

I can't.

Because I am not a victim.

Regardless of the injustices or abuse I experience, I will remember that it is because of Jesus that I have more than I'll ever need and an inheritance of eternal life! I refuse to sulk and pout about what anyone did to me.

I will only praise and rejoice in what Jesus did for me!

Just as cookies are considered little cakes, we ought to be considered little Christs.

Christ is a Victor; so are we. We have the same Spirit living in us!

Romans 8:11 says, **"The Spirit of God, who raised Jesus from the dead, lives in you. And just as God raised Christ Jesus from the dead, he will give life to your mortal bodies by this same Spirit living within you."** [11] If we share this in common with Christ, we can have the assurance that we will overcome!

The world may rise against us.

Enemies both physical and supernatural may oppose us.

When we rest under the anointing of the Holy Spirit, we can have confidence, just like Jesus, that we can endure and overcome the afflictions we face.

Paul writes it best in Romans 8:35-39.

"Who shall separate us from the love of Christ? Shall tribulation, or distress, or persecution, or famine, or nakedness, or danger, or sword? As it is written, "For your sake we are being killed all the day long; we are regarded as sheep to be slaughtered. "No, in all these things we are more than conquerors through him who loved us. For I am sure that neither death nor life, nor angels nor rulers, nor things present nor things to come, nor powers, nor height nor depth, nor anything else in all creation, will be able to separate us from the love of God in Christ Jesus our Lord." [12]

When we live like Jesus, we live like we are winning, because we are!

LIVE LIKE YOU'RE WINNING

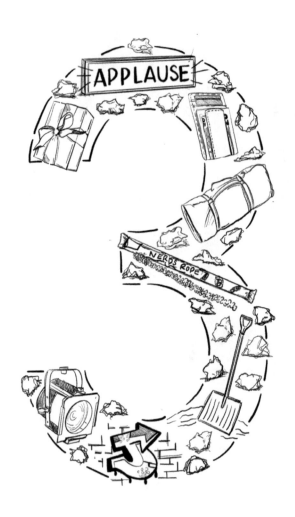

CURTAIN CALLS

LITTLE PIECES

OF PAPER

LOOK FOR LITTLE PIECES OF PAPER

CHAPTER 3

LOOK FOR LITTLE PIECES OF PAPER

Back story time!

I am a theater kid.

I've been in my fair share of productions as an actor and director. Theater has always been special to me. My first role ever was at a production at my church. It was a kid's Christmas play titled after a Dr. Seuss book. I was playing the role of a young homeless boy named Pete. I had a few lines. I sang a song or two.

Honestly, all I can remember about this production is waiting in the wings with my friend and delivering my lines from the side of the stage.

I learned quickly, and at a young age, after you perform for people, you stand on the stage under the spotlight and bow. Better yet, after you bow, they applaud you! (I hadn't learned about boo's yet).

The bows are known as the Curtain Call.

This became my favorite part of the whole show. I loved the applause.

I especially loved standing ovations. Those moments are unlike any other!

I loved having my hard work and talent recognized. I loved compelling people to stand to their feet. It's a rewarding experience; one, only stage performers will ever truly understand.

When I was a kid, I had the best kids pastor ever, Pastor Neil.

He was the gentlest, most loving, and fun kid's pastor in the world. One Sunday morning in kid's church, he got up on the stage and started talking about serving. He talked about how when we serve people we ought to do so without seeking applause. This message was tough for me to hear.

"But applause is the best part!" I muttered to myself. Then he went even further. He told a story about Jesus in the Bible. He taught about doing things because they are right, not to get accolades.

I twiddled my thumbs in my seat. He quoted Jesus and said that it is better to give than to receive and something about not doing your good deeds in front of others to gain recognition.

Sound familiar?

Once I saw the scripture on the screen, I knew I should pay attention. After all, if Jesus was into selflessly serving people, it couldn't be that bad of an idea.
I don't remember the rest of the sermon; but I do remember what happened at the end.

Pastor Neil pulled out a Nerds Rope.

This candy was relatively new in the early 2000's and I loved them! They are essentially a string of strawberry licorice covered in nerds candy pieces. He held the candy in the air and said, "But remember, God is always watching you. And he notices the good things you do in secret. One day, he will reward you." I was intrigued. Where was he going with this? I started thinking about how I could earn this Nerds Rope. What could I do? Will I have an opportunity to do something to deserve the prize? The little actor in me was getting ready to perform!

"Earlier…" Pastor Neil continued.

"I left a small piece of paper on the floor in front of the stage. I stood back and watched. Many of you walked right past the paper without even noticing it. Others of you looked at it but didn't pick it up. But one of you stopped, picked it up, and threw it in the trash."

He then pointed right at me.

I thought, "I didn't pick up that paper."

"Josh"

Pastor Neil motioned to my older brother, sitting just to the right of me. "Come on up here."

I was shocked.

Josh did something so small, so seemingly insignificant, and he was rewarded because unbeknownst to him, someone was watching.

To this day, I bend down and pick up small pieces of paper I find on the ground.

I just can't walk past them.

For a while after that Sunday morning, I would pick up every piece of trash I could find. Not because I cared to clean up, but because I was paranoid that I would fail another secret character test. After a few decades I learned nobody is watching. I learned that most of the time, people don't notice the good things you do. Even if they do, there is no Nerds Rope in their pocket to reward you.

Colossians 3:23-24 says, **"Whatever you do, work heartily, as for the Lord and not for men, knowing that from the Lord you will receive the inheritance as your reward. You are serving the Lord**

Christ." [1]

I like the way The Message Bible paraphrases it.

"Servants, do what you're told by your earthly masters. And don't just do the minimum that will get you by. Do your best. Work from the heart for your real Master, for God, confident that you'll get paid in full when you come into your inheritance. Keep in mind always that the ultimate Master you're serving is Christ." [2]

I'm sure I miss the occasional piece of paper.

To be honest, sometimes I don't pick up the trash.

Sometimes I'm not focused on the moment or I'm in too big of a hurry. Other times, I bend down to pick up a piece of paper, and I am overwhelmed at the many others around it so I just move on. But people, who are learning to be like Jesus, aren't perfect. Sometimes we walk over a piece of paper. Sometimes we miss it. Other times we intentionally ignore the paper on the floor. There is always room for growth and error. Thank you Jesus!

It's about progress not perfection.

Life is full of tiny pieces of paper on the ground. There are a lot of things in this world that are out of place.

There are a lot of hurting people.

There are a lot of dirty floors.

The amount of little pieces of paper littering our world can be overwhelming.

How can we possibly pick up every scrap? How can we possibly address every problem in society? What does Jesus expect us to do when faced with so much trouble?

Jesus doesn't ask us to solve all these problems. He just wants us to solve the problems he tells us to solve, when he tells us to solve them.

I have a missionary friend in a country in Eurasia. He told me about his dilemma with all the street beggars in his city. There are just too many of them. He couldn't possibly help them all. If he gave away even just a dollar to every beggar on the street, he and his family would have to abandon their mission and move back to the States. So, with a compassionate heart, oftentimes he has to walk past hurting people.

What I love most about his resolution of this issue is, he didn't make a schedule or a system to follow. He doesn't give a certain percentage. He doesn't find a way to avoid the beggars. He doesn't stop carrying cash. He solved the problem in a very simple way.

When he sees a beggar, he asks God what to do.

He simply decided to be like Jesus and allow the Holy Spirit to guide him.

GENERALIZED ANSWERS PRODUCE DISINGENUOUS ACTIONS.

Believe it or not, sometimes Jesus passed by people. He healed all that came to him. True! But, he also passed by many people who were hurting and unfortunately for them, they didn't get what they needed. Jesus knew that not everyone was ready for what he offered.

Have you heard the story of Jesus at the Pool of Bethesda? We read about it in John 5.

"Now there is in Jerusalem by the Sheep Gate a pool, in Arama-

ic called Bethesda, which has five roofed colonnades. In these lay a multitude of invalids—blind, lame, and paralyzed. One man was there who had been an invalid for thirty-eight years. When Jesus saw him lying there and knew that he had already been there a long time, he said to him, "Do you want to be healed?" The sick man answered him, "Sir, I have no one to put me into the pool when the water is stirred up, and while I am going another steps down before me." Jesus said to him, "Get up, take up your bed, and walk." And at once the man was healed, and he took up his bed and walked." [3]

John 5:2-9 ESV

Jesus walked by the pool that was surrounded with hurting people who needed a miracle. But one stuck out to Jesus. There was one person, incapable of getting to the pool when the waters were stirred. Jesus saw him. Jesus had compassion on this man. So, without making a scene, he healed the man and then slipped away. He didn't make a spectacle. He just dipped in and out.

There were people all around him who could have used a touch from God. Jesus passed them by. Jesus wasn't burdened by every person at the pool that day. He was burdened for one. He knew his responsibility wasn't to solve every problem in the colonnades.

His responsibility was to be led by the Spirit to the one who was desperate and open to receive.

My friend found a beautiful, Christ-like balance.

He submitted to the Holy Spirit's guidance rather than his own emotion. He trusts that the Holy Spirit will prompt him to give to the people who are ready to receive.

Just like Jesus.

When we do our best to be like Jesus, we notice things around us. We notice people who need help. We notice the graffiti on the bridges. We notice the snow in our neighbor's driveway.

Our mission is simple.

Would Jesus give money to the poor every time?

Would Jesus spend his days scrubbing graffiti off of bridges?

Would Jesus shovel your neighbor's driveway?

These are all questions we want a quick overarching answer to. But we can't settle for general answers to individual questions. Generalized answers produce disingenuous actions.

Jesus prefers to give people customized gifts, wrapped in their favorite color wrapping paper, rather than boring pre-written universal cards in plain white envelopes.

Jesus loves to be specific to the individual in front of him. We should too.

I can't tell you how many times I have heard people express how they were sitting in a church service and felt like the pastor was preaching right to them

I couldn't count the amount of times I've been praying for someone who shared with me afterward that I was praying exactly what they needed.

I've experienced this individual ministry of the Holy Spirit every day of my life. God has a desire to be personally and intimately involved with every precious person he has created. He sees us. He knows what we need. Jesus reminds us in Matthew 6 that God knows exactly what we need before we even ask! How?

He is paying attention.

He is paying close attention.

I can almost hear him answer me with the same two beautiful words every time I share my worry with him.

"I know."

Which means I see you. I'm watching. I'm paying attention to every detail.

If we really want to be like Jesus, we need to understand how incredibly aware he is of those around him. There is not one person whose needs are not noticed by the Father. He knows.

We are busy people. We are hurried. Worse yet, we know it. We are aware of our hurried and frantic lifestyles.

A friend asks you, "How are you?"

You respond, "Tired"

Familiar?

Our lives are packed full of things to do.

This hurried way of living doesn't only wreak havoc on our personal well-being. Hurry suppresses our ability to be mindfully aware of the needs of those around us. If we want to be like Jesus, we need to slow ourselves down to notice others.

Sunday mornings can get pretty busy. A few months ago I noticed myself frantically running around the church on Sunday mornings.

While I speed-walk around the church, I run into people. Or, and I'm embarrassed to admit this, but I would squeeze through doors past people. Unless I am actively practicing awareness, I will nudge my way through people so I can cut a second or two off of the time it takes me to accomplish whatever I'm doing.

I found myself saying "Ope, Sorry" more than "Good Morning!" and "How are you?"

It takes a little bit of self reflection to truly evaluate how hurried you are. I decided to take a little longer accomplishing the tasks at hand while being polite and loving with the people I encounter.

I'd rather be slow and aware than quick and rude.

The first step to becoming aware of those around us is to slow down.

When you notice something out of order, see a person in need, or notice a little piece of paper on the ground, take the time to listen for what the Holy Spirit is instructing you to do.

More often than not, God is cool with you picking up scraps of paper off the floor.

Jesus was compelled often not by an agenda, but by love.

There is something special about slowing down to notice the needs around us.

Maybe it's because of my theater experience, but when I'm sure no one is around to see it, I like to think of bending down to pick up that little piece of paper as a curtain call for an audience of one.

God notices every time you bend down, or should I say bow down to pick up even the tiniest piece of paper on the ground. He notices every person you take time to love. He notices every driveway you shovel and every square inch of graffiti you scrub off of a bridge.

Even though nobody else may see it, you can be sure Jesus is giving you a standing ovation from Heaven with a nerds rope in his hand.

WITCHES
WEED(S)
SEEDS

SHARE THE STORY OF GOD

CHAPTER 4

SHARE THE STORY OF GOD

There is a parable Jesus tells in Matthew 13:1-9 that I find fascinating! It is about the importance of stories and communicating.

Take a look.

"That same day Jesus went out of the house and sat beside the sea. And great crowds gathered about him, so that he got into a boat and sat down. And the whole crowd stood on the beach. And he told them many things in parables, saying: "A sower went out to sow. And as he sowed, some seeds fell along the path, and the birds came and devoured them. Other seeds fell on rocky ground, where they did not have much soil, and immediately they sprang up, since they had no depth of soil, but when the sun rose they were scorched. And since they had no root, they withered away. Other seeds fell among thorns, and the thorns grew up and choked them. Other seeds fell on good soil and produced grain, some a hundredfold, some sixty, some thirty. He who has ears, let him hear." [1]

Matthew 13:1-9 ESV

Jesus tells stories.

That's how he spreads seeds. He isn't as concerned about whether or not the people he talks to actually understand what he is saying as he is with the objective of sharing the story. That's not his job. His job is to spread the seeds.

Jesus uses stories as his primary communication strategy. He relies on the Holy Spirit to speak to hearts.

He does his job and steps back.

Many times, we try to over explain things. The truths of God are not revealed to people by our articulation. The truths of God are revealed by the Holy Spirit's revelation. Jesus knows this simple fact.

The disciples asked him why he spoke in confusing parables in verse 10-13.

Believe it or not, Jesus gave them a straightforward answer.

Often, in the Gospels, Jesus answers his disciples in another parable or another question. Rarely does Jesus give a direct answer to a question, but here, he is clear. His reason is important.

"And he answered them, "To you it has been given to know the secrets of the kingdom of Heaven, but to them it has not been given. Whoever has will be given more, and they will have an abundance. Whoever does not have, even what they have will be taken from them. This is why I speak to them in parables, because seeing they do not see, and hearing they do not hear, nor do they understand. Indeed, in their case the prophecy of Isaiah is fulfilled that says: "You will indeed hear but never understand, and you will indeed see but never perceive." For this people's heart has grown dull, and with their ears they can barely hear, and their eyes they have closed, lest they should see with their eyes and hear with their ears and understand with their heart and turn, and I would heal them.' But blessed are your eyes, for they see, and your ears, for they hear." [2]

Matthew 13:11-16 ESV

This is so important to understand.

It's a paradigm for understanding that is based not in our own intellect but the Spirit's revelation.

You are NOT smart enough to understand the parables that Jesus teaches.

You are NOT wise enough to discern the hidden meanings within the scriptures.

You are NOT brilliant enough to perfectly interpret the original intent of the authors.

Nobody is!

And nobody is expected to be!

It's up to the Holy Spirit to speak revelation to our minds.

We don't figure it out; it is revealed to us. This is why Jesus speaks in often confusing and challenging parables. He intentionally hides truth from those who are too proud to seek after it. Look at who didn't understand the things Jesus said. There were only two groups of people who didn't get it.

They were the Pharisees and the spectators. They didn't understand because they weren't genuinely seeking truth. They were seeking their own agenda. Those who seek their own agenda in the scriptures will not gain understanding, but lose what little they had. The Lord would rather have you know nothing than something that promotes your selfish desires.

The Pharisees were knowledgeable of the scriptures, but they couldn't see the Messiah who was right in front of them. Jesus confused them because they made their law their lord. They didn't humbly approach the scriptures to seek the Spirit's revelation. They opened the scrolls so they could open their mouths. They were arrogant. They benefited from the head knowledge they had.

It made them rich and powerful.

The account of Nicodemus in John 3 shows us the tension the religious leaders lived in. Some of them were so far gone; they had no grasp on truth. They were completely blinded to God. They were deaf to his voice. But Nicodemus was humble. He wasn't perfect, but he was humble enough to seek after the truth. He was humble enough to learn from someone else. And to him, Jesus revealed the way of God.

The second group of people, the Spectators, are those who love their own life too much. If they could just go do something first, then they'd follow Jesus. If they could still keep their money, their power, their family and friends, they would follow Jesus. We read about these people in Luke 9.

"As they were going along the road, someone said to him, "I will follow you wherever you go." And Jesus said to him, "Foxes have holes, and birds of the air have nests, but the Son of Man has nowhere to lay his head." To another he said, "Follow me." But he said, "Lord, let me first go and bury my father." And Jesus said to him, "Leave the dead to bury their own dead. But as for you, go and proclaim the kingdom of God. Yet another said, "I will follow you, Lord, but let me first say farewell to those at my home." Jesus said to him, "No one who puts his hand to the plow and looks back is fit for the kingdom of God." [3]

Luke 9:57-62 ESV

These people followed Jesus publicly but weren't willing to count the costs and follow him personally. They followed Jesus to get food or entertainment. They followed him to be in with the crowds, to be a part of the movement. They followed Jesus to benefit their selfish desires. They followed Jesus around because it made them feel good. Jesus' parables go right over their heads.

In Matthew 9:36 these people are referred to as sheep without a shepherd. They followed but didn't submit themselves to the leadership and authority of Jesus. The words the shepherd (Jesus) speaks to them go in one ear and out the other.

Jesus speaks about the kingdom in a way that goes beyond human understanding. The truth is hidden so that the Holy Spirit is the only one who can reveal it. It's like Jesus gives you a box with your answers inside, but a lock is keeping it shut. That seems unfair, but it's not.

The Holy Spirit holds the key and all you need to do is ask him to unlock it.

It is important to note that people remember stories.

In Jesus' culture and time period, stories were all many people had. Most of the people Jesus taught were illiterate and uneducated.

WE DON'T PICK AND CHOOSE WHOM WE SHARE THIS GOSPEL WITH. IT'S NOT UP TO US. WE TELL THE STORY TO THE AUDIENCE IN FRONT OF US.

Jesus knew that if he were to publish a book and hand it out along with the fishes and loaves, the words in print would only go so far. Likewise, Jesus knew that the instructions and teachings he was presenting would go in one ear and out the other. Given time, many of his incredibly valuable teachings would simply be forgotten.

Carmine Gallo notes the value of storytelling in his book Talk Like Ted,

"Scientists have produced a mountain of evidence showing back concepts presented as pictures instead of words are more likely to be recalled. Put simply, visuals matter – a lot. If you hear information, you are likely to remember about 10 percent of that information three days later. Add a picture, however, and your recall rate will soar to 65 percent. To put that in context, a picture will help you remember six times more information than listening to the words alone." [4]

Talk Like Ted, pp. 213

Jesus knew exactly what he was doing when he coupled his teachings with stories. These parables taught the truths about the kingdom of God in a way that would likely be recalled.

This is the key to Jesus' teachings.

He knew the retention rate of his stories would far surpass the next few days of his audience's busy lives. Jesus knew that the listeners would likely encounter situations similar to the stories he told.

They would see a sower sowing seeds and remember the parable.

They would see someone building a house on a stone foundation and remember the parable.

They would lose a coin and remember the parable.

They would see a shepherd and remember the parable.

They would inevitably think about these stories again.

And you can count on the Holy Spirit to be there the next time someone thinks about that parable and is humble enough to ask the question,

"What does this mean?"

The Holy Spirit is just waiting for that one moment of humility and he will capitalize on it when it comes.

Through the parables, God's hidden truths are preserved in the psyche of the listener for a far greater amount of time.

Jesus doesn't stress over who got the message. He doesn't worry about whether or not he communicated well enough.

He knows what he is doing.

He just presents the Gospel in story form and lives a life in step with the Father; the rest is up to the Holy Spirit. He knows he planted a seed. He knows that in time, those he loves so desperately might remember his stories and seek the truth.

I had an epiphany one day early in my career as a pastor. I would get so upset about how apathetically people were responding to the Gospel.

I would spend nights crying out to God to save these people I loved so much. I heard God say, "Casey, don't you think I want them to be saved a little more than you?"

I was getting so frustrated with how long it was taking them to understand simple kingdom principles. It didn't even cross my mind that maybe they weren't ready. My job is not to bring revelation; it is to share the story of God and watch the Holy Spirit stir a response in people's lives. Some people don't respond immediately.

I could tell you story after story of people I barely know telling me about "that one time" I told them something, and it changed their life. I can't tell you what I said.

I don't remember.

All I know is that when I talk to people, I want to tell the story of God just like Jesus did. People will respond in their time.

Some people respond quickly and grow strong but the weeds around them choke them out.

Some people, sadly, never respond to the Gospel because they live in the barren desert of pride and self-indulgence.

Some people grow deep roots and become strong Jesus people!

My job is to scatter the seed. It is the Holy Spirit's job to bring revelation.

Jesus knew that there were people in the audience who would never understand. He knew there would be some bandwagon fans that followed for a bit. He also knew that there would be a few who would be humble enough to receive the revelation from the Holy Spirit.

We don't pick and choose whom we share this Gospel with. It's not up to us. We tell the story to the audience in front of us.

One afternoon, while teaching an evangelism class, a couple students and I made the voyage to Wal-Mart. We asked God who we should pray for and if he would identify them to us. Sure enough, we found a couple people matching the descriptions of the people we felt we heard God describe.

This is a fun exercise to do. It breaks you out of your comfort zone. It forces you to rely on the Holy Spirit's ever-so small voice.

This day became one I doubt I'll ever forget. One of my students felt like God was leading them to a person wearing a green jacket.

As we walked through the isles, we came across a man wearing a jacket with Marijuana leaves patterned over the back.

"That's green", I thought.

The boys I was with noticed as well and we agreed that it was worth a shot. What's the worst that could happen? We share the Gospel with the wrong person? I didn't think that was possible...

...until he introduced us to his mom.

He was a kind guy, probably in his early twenties. It seemed like he was just a little high while we were talking to him. (Not surprising.)

We started sharing with him the story of God.

We told him we'd love to pray with him for whatever he may need, right there in the men's clothing department.

That's when he said, "You guys need to pray for my mom!"

He called his mom over to us. It seemed like she was hiding behind the racks of clothes as she moved closer to us like a snake weaving her way through the grass. She definitely gave off a creepy vibe.

We smiled and asked her if she needed prayer.

She didn't tell us her life story.

She didn't say she had back pain.

She didn't complain about her son's drug problems.

She just calmly said,

"I'm a witch."

"Oh, Ok." I responded as I took a deep breath.

The students next to me took a step back.

"Does that scare you?" she asked.

"Not at all." I told her.

"It scares them." She said as she motioned to my students who were drifting further and further away.

"No, it doesn't." I said as I pulled them back to my side. "They're fine."

There was an awkward pause. "You know your aura is crazy right now. You need to chill." She said as she handed me something.

I looked at the pink piece of resin she placed in my hand.

"That's a rose crystal. It will calm down your aura."

I laughed, "Nothing will calm me down. I'll only shine brighter."
She respected my response.

I talked with this woman and her son for a few minutes.

She had questions. I had answers.

She thought I was crazy. (The feeling was mutual.)

But after some conversation, she actually let us pray for her.

We asked God to show her how much he loved her. We prayed that she would find him. We prayed that she would have a humble heart to hear the Holy Spirit. We reminded her that God loves her. We shared the story of God, parted ways, and trusted the Holy Spirit do his job.

It was definitely a weird situation.

It was very uncomfortable.

I didn't really want to share the Gospel with this self-proclaimed witch.

I certainly didn't want to hold her hand and pray with her and her half-baked son.

But, as the conversations went further and further, this woman started looking a lot more like a plant being choked by a thistle than a witch. I felt compassion for her. I knew if that weed could be uprooted, she would be able to thrive in Christ! I knew the seed could grow.

My prayers began to focus more on removing the weeds. Judging by the woman's demeanor both before and after our conversation and prayers, she definitely encountered God.

Sometimes, God leads you to the guy with weed on his jacket so he can remove the weeds from his mom's heart.

Stranger things have happened.

I saw the woman in Wal-Mart three times after our initial conversation.

Each time, I waved and smiled.

She shook her head like I was crazy and then smiled back.

She reminded me of Wendy Peffercorn from the classic movie
The Sandlot. She waved at me like Wendy waved at Squints.
I could tell she felt valued. I could tell that wasn't a normal feeling
for her. I could tell she actually appreciated what we had shared
with her. She may have thought I was crazy, but she respected
what I had done for her.

Did she end up ditching the darkness of witchcraft and choose
to follow Jesus?

I don't know.

I will one day.

I'm praying she will find herself in a humble enough place where
the Holy Spirit can lead her to Jesus.

But that is not my job.

I just tell stories. I just sow the seeds.

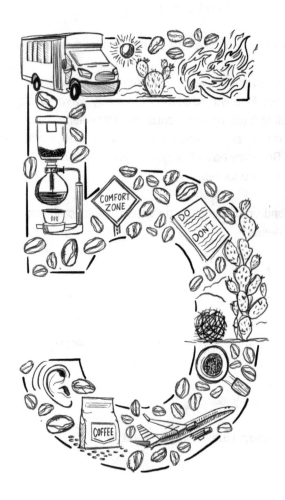

COFFEE
DESERTS
CAB RIDES

BE PATIENT IN THE DESERT

CHAPTER 5

BE PATIENT IN THE DESERT

I have been in love with coffee for a while now.

I started drinking coffee in the Blue Mountains of Jamaica while on a missions trip in High School. Jamaican Blue Mountain Coffee is considered some of the best coffee in the world. The high altitude and plenty of sunlight create the perfect environment to grow coffee. Specifically, the high altitude means that there is less oxygen. Less oxygen makes it more difficult for coffee plants to grow the coffee beans we all know and love. So, the coffee plant needs to work extra hard in order to grow the little fruits. Low oxygen plus hard work creates lactic acid. This lactic acid causes the beans to taste less bitter and creamier. The flavor is not as harsh and is actually really enjoyable, even without cream and sugar. I had a cup of this coffee in Jamaica and I noticed the difference immediately. It was much better than the store brand pre-ground coffee I had at home. I started craving this coffee. By the end of the week I was a full fledged coffee addict.

Still am.

I had to stop drinking coffee for a diet I was doing once and I thought I was going to die.

I remember going into my friend Scott's office for a meeting at church. I don't remember what happened, all I remember is waking up on the couch in his office. I've since significantly reduced the number of cups, or should I say pots of coffee I drink on a daily basis. Now, I try my best to restrict my consumption to just a few cups a day. So, I make them count. I want to drink the best coffee money can buy. And when possible, I prefer to brew at home.

Many people identify me as a pretentious coffee snob. Though I don't think this is the most accurate term to define my coffee interests, I get it. I am someone who appreciates artisan small batch, single origin coffee the same way one would appreciate a painting by Monet or Degas. Does that make me sound even more pretentious? I'll deal with it...

I have about a dozen different brew methods in my home.

My favorite of which is a siphon brewer my mom bought me for my birthday one year. If you don't know what that is, check out some videos online and appreciate it for a second. It looks like an evil chemist's preferred brew method. Or just check it out in the sketch for chapter five!

Though I brew coffee nearly every day, I had not roasted it until recently. There are a few ways to roast coffee at home. I chose to learn by hand in a small circular ceramic pot.

When I use the roasting pot, I imagine myself in the outback of Australia roasting coffee for an aboriginal tribe. Roasting coffee is a fascinating practice. It is incredibly simple, almost too simple. Despite its simplicity, when trying to replicate flavors, it becomes a minute science. So many roasters around the world have nearly perfected this science.

I am not one of those people. The pros have gotten this process down pat. They can calibrate their roast to the exact temperature, tumble, weight, air quality, exhaust, etc. They have thought of everything. But, if you are an amature coffee roaster like me and you want to give it a shot, you only have to know how to do one thing.

Listen.

This is the key.

When roasting coffee by hand I have almost zero chance of yielding a consistent roast time and time again. I can't control the temperature perfectly. I can't agitate the beans the same way twice. Because of this, I learned to listen for the cue.

It's kind of like singing in a choir or having a solo in a musical. You have to listen for your cue. That cue is called the first crack. The first crack happens when nearly all the moisture has escaped the bean along with coffee's good friend CO_2. The bean expands and then cracks. It sounds a lot like popcorn.

It's a big sound compared to the relative silence of tumbling beans in a pot. The first crack is very noticeable. And just like popcorn, the first crack becomes less frequent. As that happens, you start to hear smaller crackles. This is the second crack.

At this point in the roasting process, the coffee bean is beginning to break down. The small cracks are signifying the darkening of the coffee. I usually stop around this point because I like a medium roast. Another reason I stop here is because I'm always afraid I will burn the beans.

Nevertheless, now you know how to roast coffee! Congratulations! It will also help to read a lot of blogs. (Coffee geeks are notorious bloggers.)

The roasting process is simple.

Put the beans over the fire, agitate them, listen, and then remove the beans from the fire.

There's not much to it.

Just listen and respond accordingly.

I think Jesus lived this way.

I think he listened more than he listed.

Instead of making lists of do's and don'ts, Jesus lived his life in a way that made sure he was always listening to the Holy Spirit.

THE SEASONS IN THE DESERT ARE IMPORTANT. THEY ARE PRODUCING QUALITIES IN YOU THAT ARE UNATTAINABLE INSIDE YOUR COMFORT ZONE.

Let's look at Matthew 4:1,

"Then Jesus was led up by the Spirit into the wilderness to be tempted by the devil." [1]

Matthew 4:1 ESV

The Holy Spirit led Jesus into a challenge. These next forty days would not be pleasant, but they would be important. Jesus spent forty days and nights fasting in the wilderness. After the last day, the devil stopped by to tempt Jesus. Matthew seems to suggest that this temptation would be the main reason for Jesus' journey into the wilderness.

The forty days and nights of fasting had a purpose. They were used to cause Jesus to desire nothing more than food and comfort.

Fasting teaches us what it feels like to only crave our fleshly desires while we practice neglecting them instead of indulging them. It trains us to say no to things that are lesser and yes to the things of God.

Jesus was pushed to the breaking point, but Jesus still didn't break. The devil offered Jesus bread, he offered Jesus servants, and he offered Jesus power and authority. Jesus rejected each one of these carnal desires. Jesus was given three chances to escape his forty-day trek of deprivation, and he remained steadfast.

Why?

I don't believe Jesus was going anywhere until he heard the Holy Spirit tell him to move. Luke 4:14 tells us what Jesus did immediately following the temptation, **"And Jesus returned in the power of the Spirit to Galilee..."** [2]

Jesus would not leave his trial until the Holy Spirit said it was time.

He would endure every torment and temptation until the Holy Spirit said it was time to move.

I have found myself in seasons of trial and temptation time after time. If Jesus had to go through it, I believe we need to as well. I don't believe these seasons are punishments. What would Jesus have been punished for? He had never done anything wrong. So, if a perfect man had to endure a season of depravity and temptations where everything within him just wanted to escape; how much more should we? There is a reason for the trial. When we lose something, it's almost instantaneous that the tempter comes around to offer a counterfeit.

We can't give in.

Staying faithful in these seasons develops us.

If Jesus had to develop, you better believe that we have to!

Lou Engle says,

"Prophets are formed out of the deserts of fasting not the desserts of feasting." [3]

We need to get to a place in our walk with Jesus where we value deserts over desserts. It's easy to get caught up in the enjoyment of material things. Enjoying material things isn't bad. But, when we value our comfort, our material things, our emotional gratifications over embracing the desert, we never fully develop into a Christ-like individual.

Deserts

Desserts

If we rush out of the desert seasons too soon, we run the risk of being under developed, unequipped, and maybe even bitter. That's what happens to coffee. If you don't listen for the first and second crack, if you take it off too early, it will taste terrible. Raw coffee beans taste like grass. Burnt coffee tastes like charcoal. Perfectly roasted coffee tastes just right.

If we leave the fire too soon, we won't gain the necessary qualities God is developing in us. If we leave too late, we may get burnt.

Our seasons of suffering are not just random seasons.

God is using the fire to draw out the dross and refine us. He wants us to endure the suffering and wait for the Holy Spirit to direct us when it is time to step out of our pain and into his power. Romans 5:3-4 says, **"Not only that, but we rejoice in our sufferings, knowing that suffering produces endurance, and endurance produces character, and character produces hope," [4]**

The seasons in the desert are important. They are producing qualities in you that are unattainable inside your comfort zone.

I know the desert seasons don't seem beneficial while we are in them. But be encouraged! As someone who has gone through a few desert seasons and has come out in the power of the Holy Spirit, just wait for the cue before you leave.

Wait for the Holy Spirit to clearly speak to you what your next step may be.

Don't take yourself out of the fire too soon.

Don't stay in too long.

Listen for the crack.

And don't we just feel like we are about to crack during these seasons?

I think we are. It's important that we do, because nobody wants a raw or burnt cup of coffee, especially if you are a pretentious coffee addict like me.

Regardless of your coffee affinity, we are all called to wait for the Holy Spirit's leading.

The desert is a wasteland. It is a place where you have no control. You have no resources. You have little to no hope.

———

I love to travel.

I'm too tall to love planes... but the temporary pain of having my knees pressed up against the seat in front of me for hours on end is worth the travel experience.

I was taking a solo trip to Israel. I had never been to Israel prior to that trip. So, I was a little nervous and unsure about where exactly I was going. I got off the plane in Tel Aviv and was immediately greeted, (and I use that term lightly) by a customs agent. After the tense questioning from the customs agent at the gate, I realized the tensions were high in this country; higher than I expected.

I made it through the checkpoint and walked out of the airport. I had no idea what to do next. I thought finding a ride to my hotel would be a good place to start. I didn't find any Uber. There were no yellow taxis. There were only a handful of sketchy minibuses lined up along the curb.

The drivers were all competing for business with the enthusiasm of carnival game hosts. I looked around for another American to see if anyone knew if these guys were credible drivers and not just kidnappers. I found a few other travelers who were just as confused as I was. We all decided to take the risk together.

If it all went south, at least we had each other.

I sat in the minibus that was supposed to take me to Jerusalem waiting for other passengers. None of us knew what was going on. Someone would stick their head in the door and ask, "Is this bus going to Jerusalem?" We'd all look around at each other and say, "Hope so." We began our trip.

It was something like an hour drive to get to my hotel. The man driving didn't really acknowledge us the entire time he was with us. The only thing I remember him saying was, "We are switching drivers."

Uh, what?

He pulled over on the side of the desert highway. Everyone in the bus was becoming visibly disturbed. We watched as the driver got out and handed the keys to another man standing on the side of a parked car. I looked for an exchange of money. I was both concerned that I was being sold and curious as to how much I was being sold for. The new driver got in the driver's seat and got us back on the road.

The new driver got in the front seat and started up the minibus. I just sat there waiting. I had no idea what was going on.

Was I ever going to make it to Jerusalem? I looked around me to see nothing but desert mountains. It's no wonder the Israelites got lost there for forty years!

When you're in the desert, it is easy to lose track of where you are heading.

Everything seemed fine. But the tension in the shuttle was tangible. It got even more stressful as he pulled out his phone and started dialing a number. He rested the phone on his shoulder and cocked his head in place to hold it steady.

This was a necessary step for our shuttle driver because, well... he only had one hand.

I know, our unknown, one-handed chauffeur was speeding through the desert highway while talking on his cell phone.

Did I mention the vehicle was a stick shift?

I sat still behind the driver watching how he held up the phone with his handless arm against his cheek as he simultaneously reached over with his hand to shift gears, while steering with his knees.

At this point in the trip, I was more impressed than concerned about my safety. If this was the end, so be it. If I live, I've got a good story to tell.

When we arrived in Jerusalem, I don't know if I've ever been more relieved and excited to be somewhere. The city was beautiful. I never imagined it being this wonderful. I got out of the minibus and thanked the driver.

Though my ride through the desert was sketchy and scary,
and at times confusing, I made it.

The desert seasons we face are a lot like my ride into Jerusalem.

Confusing.

Scary.

And full of surprises.

But, as we learn to endure these desert seasons and learn what we are there to learn, the desert becomes a sacred space. We gain a new appreciation for all that sand.

I am reminded of the Desert Fathers.

These early church monastics would retreat to the desert so that they could learn to deny themselves of worldly things and embrace counter-cultural things like silence, focus, and solitude.

They embraced the desert.

Their faith grew stronger as a result.

They learned to be silent and listen to the Holy Spirit.

The prayers that came out of the sanctuaries of these deserted monastics are some of the most brilliant contemplative prayers that have been uttered by human tongues.

I am reminded of Paul, who escaped to the desert to learn from the sacred sands of solitude.

"For I would have you know, brothers, that the gospel that was preached by me is not man's gospel. For I did not receive it from any man, nor was I taught it, but I received it through a revelation of Jesus Christ. For you have heard of my former life in Judaism, how I persecuted the church of God violently and tried to destroy it. And I was advancing in Judaism beyond many of my own age among my people, so extremely zealous was I for the traditions of my fathers. But when he who had set me apart before I was born, and who called me by his grace, was pleased to reveal his Son to me, in order that I might preach him among the Gentiles, I did not immediately consult with anyone; nor did I go up to Jerusalem to those who were apostles before me, but I went away into Arabia, and returned again to Damascus." [5]

Galatians 1:11-17 ESV

Paul spent time in solitude to be taught about the Gospel by Jesus. No wonder the Pauline epistles carry so much authority. No wonder this author was so effectively used to write and instruct the churches in the way of faith. Paul spent time embracing the desert. He sought the wisdom only God could give in the location only he could truly hear.

I am reminded of King David, who fled the harsh treatment of King Saul and chose to live in the desert caves rather than a palace. King David was "a man after God's own heart".

How?

Just a quick recap of David's life will prove he had certainly fallen short of God's glory just like everyone else. Yet, he did at least one thing right; and that led to success unknown to anyone before him.

David embraced the desert.

Out of his desert seasons we get many of the beautiful psalms we still read and memorize today. This stanza seems appropriate to highlight.

"O God, you are my God; earnestly I seek you; my soul thirsts for you; my flesh faints for you, as in a dry and weary land where there is no water." [6]

Psalm 63:1 ESV

I also think of the words of the great Jedi Master Yoda when talking to Master Obi Wan Kenobi after the defeat of the evil Galactic Empire.

Before Master Kenobi flees with the infant Luke Skywalker to the desert planet of Tatooine, Yoda stops him and says, "In your solitude on Tatooine, training I have for you."

Even our fictional Jedi heroes understand the importance of desert seasons. Obi Wan Kenobi was sent to the desert to become stronger and more mature in the ways of the force. As Christians, we retreat to the desert to become stronger and more mature in the way of the faith.

The desert is a sacred space.It is an inevitable reality that we spend a season, even if it may be brief, in the desert of our soul. In this desert we learn to thirst for the Lord. We learn where our strength is found. We learn who is our sustainer and provider. It is and will only be Jesus.

The desert is not comfortable, but it is necessary.

Remember to listen for the cue to come out of the desert in the power of the Holy Spirit.

Embrace the desert, don't escape the desert.

Embrace the desert like

The Desert Fathers

The Apostle Paul

King David

Master Obi Wan Kenobi

Most importantly...

Embrace the desert like Jesus.

BE PATIENT IN THE DESERT

LEADERSHIP

CANYONS

FOLLOWING

FOCUS ON FOLLOWING

CHAPTER 6

FOCUS ON FOLLOWING

What does it look like to lead?

John Maxwell is perhaps the most notable and popular leadership guru of our time. He has this to say about leadership,

"Leadership is not about titles, positions or flowcharts. It is about one life influencing another." [1]

What a great definition.

Leadership is influence!

If we just leave it there, I think we can all walk away with a basic understanding of leadership.

Early in my career, I understood that leadership was influence, but the question still gnawed at my mind like a rabbit on a carrot;

"How do I become a leader?"

or

"How do I become influential?"

This question is profound. It leads us down the road of self-discovery. It leads us on a never-ending quest to become the most positively influential people we can be; ultimately allowing us the platform to change the world for the better.

This is what we all want, right?

We all want to change the world! Or at least, our small part of it.

Something separates a truly influential person from those who are content with squandering their potential. Leaders work hard to become someone worth following. Leaders don't just exist; they evolve.

A leader must be willing to grow and change.

To do this, most leaders I know recommend reading different leadership books, or attending conferences, or listening to podcasts focused on the disciplines of leadership.

I'm a lifelong learner. So, I read the books they recommended me.

I went to the conferences.

I listened to the podcasts.

I did the things I was advised to do.

I didn't notice much change. I felt like I was just building walls around myself. I got trapped in all the rigidity of the leadership system. I don't like feeling trapped. I felt like I was drowning in the responsibilities of my leadership position. I cried out for help. Instead of a flotation device, I was thrown an anchor. I felt alone. I felt like I wasn't cut out to be a leader. It was like I was responsible for defusing a bomb without any bright red wire to cut. Where do you even start? Everyone else I knew was getting it. All my friends were thriving. I was stuck watching from behind, just waiting for it to click.

I developed an early morning routine.

I read more blogs and listened to more leadership podcasts.

I structured my ideal workweek and managed my time.

I would put down a leadership book and feel empty. I was left want-ing. I felt like I had been jipped out of the fifteen dollars I spent on the book. I did all the stuff the authors talk about. Yet nothing changed. In fact, I felt worse. All my insecurities about my capacity as a lead-er were only affirmed by my struggles under-standing what every other leader I knew so quickly grasped.

Maybe I'm just not cut out to be a leader.

Have you ever felt this way?

Maybe you're like me. Maybe you were thrown into whatever responsibility you find yourself in and you don't know what to do.

Being in that position is no fun at all.

I know.

It is hard to feel like you're working from behind. It's hard to feel like you are incapable of doing what you need to do.

I want to encourage you in this chapter. If you can empathize with me, read closely.

There was one simple truth that changed it all for me. It came when I started focusing on how Jesus led. I noticed some trends in Jesus' ministry that created a whole new paradigm for leadership for me.

As I began to ground my understanding of leadership in the life and teachings of Jesus, I began to grow confident. I noticed areas of my ministry where I was relying on systems Jesus hadn't established. I was finding areas of my personal life that were inconsistent with the life of Jesus. As I dug deeper into the lifestyle Jesus lived, I became confident again in my ability to do what God called me to do. This chapter is for everyone who has felt like they weren't cut out for being influential. For the normal people like me, who have zero desire to run a multi-million dollar cooperation. For the people who just want to be like Jesus and positively influence the people God puts around them.

I've been a pastor since I was nineteen years old. Yeah, that's right, someone (Brooks McElhenny) hired me when I was just nineteen years old. Over these few years pastoring I've learned that being influential in the kingdom is very different than what we are taught by the world.

Pastor Brooks showed me that.

He hired a nineteen-year-old hipster on a whim. Was this a well calculated leadership move? Did Brooks just finish a book about hiring goofy millennials?

I don't know what was going on in his head.

I do know what was going on in his heart.

Brooks felt the Holy Spirit lead him. Brooks followed. He knew the simple truth we often forget as leaders. We may be called leaders, but in reality the Holy Spirit leads; we follow.

I was on a cross-country road trip from Michigan to California.

Just four friends and one Honda Civic. I was expecting to go to California and hang out with some of my best friends, surf, shoot the breeze, and relax without a care in the world.

I didn't expect to be called into ministry.

I missed his initial call because we were jamming out to what I'm sure is an incredible playlist composed of road trip songs, show tunes, and worship music. When we arrived in Kansas City, Missouri, I looked at my phone. I had a missed call from a Metro Detroit area code. There was a voicemail. When I hit play, I heard a soft-spoken southern man who had a timbre in his voice that told me he was excited, but also questioning the sanity of the phone call.

He said, (please read this in a southern accent) "Hi Casey! My name is Brooks, from Northville Christian Assembly. We are looking for a new Children's Pastor, and this may sound a little crazy but your name came up and I felt like the Holy Spirit was telling me to give you a call. Would you like to stop by for an interview?"

Seriously?

My life changed at that moment.

When people ask me when I was called into the ministry, I tell them it was when Pastor Brooks literally called me into the ministry.

One thing led to another, and I became the Children's Pastor at Northville Christian Assembly only about a month later.

Brooks was leading, but he was also following.

He heard a voice.

The voice said to call me, and he did.

Brooks followed the leading of the Holy Spirit rather than conventional wisdom. Because of this "followship", he took a shot on an uneducated, wild, insanely extroverted, diamond in the rough.

What would compel him to do that? Well, he was a diamond in the rough when he was first hired as a pastor. His story is similar to mine. Someone felt the calling of God on his life and they followed the Holy Spirit's leading. Brooks trusted that if God did it once, he could do it again.

Brooks followed.

Brooks submitted.

Brooks didn't take the Lord's advice and run it through his system to determine whether or not to heed it.

Brooks obeyed.

Brooks made sure he was focused on following.

In fact, if Pastor Brooks had submitted the instruction of the Holy Spirit to a man-made system; he probably would've missed it.

I wouldn't be writing this book right now. I doubt I would be in ministry.

But that is not my story! Instead, I am here.

Pastor Brooks chose to submit his systems to the authority of God alone!

I couldn't be more grateful.

Jesus wasn't trying to be a great leader.

In Matthew 8 we read a story about Jesus healing a man with leprosy.

"When he came down from the mountain, great crowds followed him. And behold, a leper came to him and knelt before him, saying, "Lord, if you will, you can make me clean." And Jesus stretched out his hand and touched him, saying, "I will; be clean." And immediately his leprosy was cleansed. And Jesus said to him, "See that you say nothing to anyone, but go, show yourself to the priest and offer the gift that Moses commanded, for a proof to them." [2]

Matthew 8:1-4 ESV

The first verse is important.

It sets the stage for this story.

Great crowds were following Jesus.

> **LEADERS WORK HARD TO BECOME SOMEONE WORTH FOLLOWING. LEADERS DON'T JUST EXIST; THEY EVOLVE.**

Jesus was avoiding the crowds.

He was trying to get away. As Jesus was retreating, a sick man stopped him. Jesus healed the man and immediately commanded him not to tell anyone.

If Jesus' goal were to gain a following, he would have engaged the crowd and publicly displayed this former leper for all to see.

But Jesus did the exact opposite.

Why?

Jesus was setting an example for us. In John 5:19 Jesus says that he never does anything unless the Father leads him to do it.

Influential people don't try to lead better; they try to be led better.

They don't strive to gain a following; they strive to be a follower.

They don't work to improve themselves; they work to improve others.

They don't want to be seen; they would rather remain invisible.

This is the model of influence that Jesus institutes:

Follow God before leading others.

My dad is a baseball coach. During the winter months he travels somewhere warm and coaches winter ball. Recently, he's been spending the winter in Palm Springs, California. Last winter, all us kids went out to visit him and my mom out in the desert. I was excited to catch a few rays and get some color before heading back to the never-ending Michigan winter. We wanted to spend a lot of time outdoors.

My family loves to hike.

Hiking is not only fun and centering; it's free.

So, that's what we did. Palm Springs has some beautiful canyon trails. It's not too leisurely of a stroll, but it's also not incredibly dangerous. These trails are the perfect middle ground between comfort and challenge.

As we hike through the canyons, we look for the trail markers. Sometimes they are visible signs. In some less traveled places they may be dots painted on rocks or trees. In the most desolate of trails, the markers are rocks that have been placed or stacked parallel with the trail. In those far reached places, you need to pay attention to even the smallest of details.

We follow whoever is in the lead. If the person up front says there is a hazard up ahead, you watch out for the hazard. If the person up front takes a turn, you turn. If the person up front rests, you rest. If the person up front tells you to slow down you slow down.

The leader carries a heavy responsibility.

They lead the group.

However, a good leader doesn't just lead the people behind them; they follow the trail markers in front of them.

It is one thing to have people follow you. It is an entirely different thing to lead the people who follow you in the right direction.

If the leader of the pack stops following the trail markers, the rest of the group wanders off track. There were times while hiking a particular canyon with my brothers and dad that we took the wrong route. We lost track of the trail markers and we were forced to follow our own novice sense of direction. It was at these times we had to climb over boulders and walk through streams in order to get back to the trail.

The trek gets more difficult for everyone when the leader isn't a good follower?

You can't be a great leader without being a great follower.

We must focus on being a follower.

"Hear, my son, and accept my words, that the years of your life may be many. I have taught you the way of wisdom; I have led you in the paths of uprightness. When you walk, your step will not be hampered, and if you run, you will not stumble. Keep hold of instruction; do not let go; guard her, for she is your life. Do not enter the path of the wicked, and do not walk in the way of the evil. Avoid it; do not go on it; turn away from it and pass on." [3]

Proverbs 4:10-15 ESV

There is a path that we are called to follow as individuals. Each of us needs to watch for the trail markers. Each of us needs to hear the voice of God for ourselves. Each of us need to take hold of wisdom and instruction. Because the path of the wicked is a real and looming threat for all of us.

It's easy to follow your own path.

We have to understand that people are always following us.

My grandpa would use this common phrase whenever we got out of hand. He was rarely upset that we would misbehave because of the harm it brought on us individually. He would get mad because "Monkey see, monkey do." He would be frustrated with us because we have little eyes watching our every move. Our younger siblings and cousins were going to misbehave and potentially get hurt because of what we were doing.

That simple phrase emphasizes the burden of our lives.

People are watching you.

Kids are watching you.

And kids do what they see you do. You don't have to be a pastor of a church, a coach of a team, or a business leader to have people paying attention to how you live.

Children are watching.

Jesus gives this warning, similar to my grandpa's in Matthew 18:6,

"But if anyone causes one of these little ones who believe in me to stumble, it would be better for him to have a large millstone hung around his neck and to be drowned in the depths of the sea." [4]

Be careful to stay on the right trail.

With such a heavy burden on our shoulders it is important to ask a simple question:

Why do we so easily wander away, when the cost of veering down the wrong path is so high?

Often we go off the path and lead people astray because we determine that our path is the best path.

We rely on our intellect and our instinct.

We become confident in our ability.

All it takes is the deadly thought, "I know where I'm going" to slip into our mind.

It will lead us down a debilitating path.

Another reason we find ourselves walking in the path of the wicked is because we neglect to spend time with God and hear his words and see his trail markers.

When we just do what someone else is doing, we follow the wrong path down the road to wickedness. The path of the wicked is the path that looks well trodden. It's easy to follow where everyone else has gone.

"But the path of the righteous is like the light of dawn, which shines brighter and brighter until full day. The way of the wicked is like deep darkness; they do not know over what they stumble." [5]

Proverbs 4:18-19 ESV

The path of the righteous is like a dawn compared to a deep darkness.

It's hard to see trail markers in the dark.

If you ever find yourself in a place where you aren't hearing God's voice, or you aren't seeing God's direction, stop! Don't move forward! Stay where you are and wait for the dawn. Wait for the sun to rise and follow the horizon.

Often times, we wander in the dark because we are determined to get through the difficult season. But when we wander in the dark, we wander in vain. We just go deeper into the woods. We go further away from the horizon.

Stop. Be still. Wait on the Lord.

The sun will rise. And you will be able to follow the trail markers again.

Jesus made sure he took the time to wait on God's direction.

It would've been easy for Jesus to get in the groove and do things the same way over and over.

But look what Jesus does in the following three stories.

"And as Jesus passed on from there, two blind men followed him, crying aloud, "Have mercy on us, Son of David." When he entered the house, the blind men came to him, and Jesus said to them, "Do you believe that I am able to do this?" They said to him, "Yes, Lord." Then he touched their eyes, saying, "According to your faith be it done to you." And their eyes were opened. And Jesus sternly warned them, "See that no one knows about it." But they went away and spread his fame through all that district." [6]

Matthew 9:27-31 ESV

"And they came to Bethesda. And some people brought to him a blind man and begged him to touch him. And he took the blind man by the hand and led him out of the village, and when he had spit on his eyes and laid his hands on him, he asked him, "Do you see anything?" And he looked up and said, "I see people, but they look like trees, walking." Then Jesus laid his hands on his eyes again; and he opened his eyes, his sight was restored, and

he saw everything clearly. And he sent him to his home, saying, "Do not even enter the village."" [7]

Mark 8:22-26 ESV

"As he passed by, he saw a man blind from birth. And his disciples asked him, "Rabbi, who sinned, this man or his parents, that he was born blind?" Jesus answered, "It was not that this man sinned, or his parents, but that the works of God might be displayed in him. We must work the works of him who sent me while it is day; night is coming, when no one can work. As long as I am in the world, I am the light of the world." Having said these things, he spit on the ground and made mud with the saliva. Then he anointed the man's eyes with the mud and said to him, "Go, wash in the pool of Siloam" (which means Sent). So he went and washed and came back seeing." [8]

John 9:1-7 ESV

In each of these instances, Jesus refuses to do the same thing twice.

Why?

Jesus wasn't following his system, he was following his Father.

Jesus knew that each of these people needed their miracle to be given in a different way. God doesn't give generic gifts. He individualizes every miracle.

We can get walking down the wrong trail because it's what we've always done, but Jesus institutes a way of doing ministry that is fluid and flexible. Jesus' ministry is entirely dependent on following what the Father in Heaven is leading him to do.

As we learn and grow in following the Holy Spirit's leading, we lead effectively with divine wisdom and authority.

To be a leader like Jesus, we need to learn how to follow the trail markers.

Sometimes we need to run away from the crowds and connect to the Father.

Being an influential person is a universal calling.

We all have people following us.

People look up to us. It doesn't matter if you are a leader for a living; you are and always will be living as a leader. This is a terrifying realization. When you learn that people are following you, whether you like it or not, you need to really focus on the path ahead. The more people you have following behind you on the trail, the more people you could possibly lead off a cliff!

As leaders we must not rely on our own ability to lead.

We simply can't risk the position we've been given.

We cannot take this into our own hands.

We cannot rely on our own strengths.

I know many leaders who are overwhelmed by the weight they carry. Are you someone like that? Do you fear leading your followers in the wrong direction? Do you feel the burden of the souls in your congregation? Do you feel the weight of the players on your team? Are you afraid of failure, because if you fail, so do those who you lead?

One thing I know for sure is that being someone of influence is not easy.

It takes constant work to remain humble and lowly. It takes devotion to not be carried off by the crowds and instead retreat to the outcasts. It takes courage to not allow what others say of us determine how we act.

Jesus set the example.

He followed the Holy Spirit's leading.

He was influential at the micro-level.

I don't know everything about leadership.

But I know that imitating Jesus is a good place to start.

If Jesus focused on following, so will I.

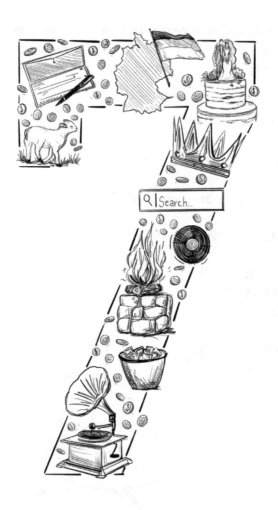

SOLOMON

ANTIQUES

MISSIONARIES

SACRIFICE FOR LOVE

CHAPTER 7

SACRIFICE FOR LOVE

I had a friend encourage me to dive into Song of Solomon. I had always known this book to be about a man's love for his bride. It's a good book to read if you want to be a good husband. So, given my relationship status at the time, I was not intrigued. I wasn't concerned with how to be a good husband. I didn't see why I needed to study how a man should love a woman. How would this love letter help me be like Jesus?

My friend knew I was questioning this book's potential impact. I was single and didn't believe the book had much relevancy to me in my life. She said, "Whenever Solomon is talking about how much he loves his bride, picture Jesus saying those things about you." I remained skeptical. I knew enough about Song of Solomon to know that it got pretty PG-13 pretty quick. I decided to pass over the eroticism and get right to the message of this love letter. I learned that Jesus really, really, really loves his bride. I found that there are actually a lot of similarities between Song of Solomon and the Gospel. Solomon loved his bride like Christ loves the Church.

As I read it, I wept. I learned a new depth of love. The Holy Spirit breathed on the words written in this love letter and it taught me of Christ's love for us, his bride.

I was surprised to feel the impact of this seemingly irrelevant book.

I'm afraid we often toss out things we don't believe are relevant to us.

In doing so, we may throw out a hidden message the Holy Spirit is patiently waiting to breathe on. Remember Chapter 4?

Jesus hides messages for us to find.

Are we ignoring potential solutions to our present problems because we have erroneously discerned the vessel of the message to be irrelevant?

I sat down with a friend for coffee to talk about ministry. She is a pastor at a small rural church of about twenty people. She shared with me her passion for these people. Twenty people don't necessarily constitute a large church. But you don't have to be a large church to have a large impact. Twenty Jesus followers praying together week after week does much more for the kingdom than a church of twenty thousand entertained fans.

We measure a church's success based on numbers. We look at the physical to gauge a spiritual body. A praying church of twenty could be the reason for the lowering of abortion rates, decreased opioid deaths, and fewer fatherless homes.

A church's success can't be measured simply based on the number of people in a pew. A church's success is measured by the number of people in prayer.

We talked about the power of prayer. We talked about how prayer has become irrelevant to many people. We have more information than anyone in the history of the world. Why do we need to ask an invisible God for answers when we can just look it up?

Prayer seems obsolete to an instant access culture. But it isn't.

Spending time in prayer is not antiquated, it's anointed!

Silence, meditation, contemplative prayer, fasting, solitude, just to name a few; are some of the most seemingly irrelevant treasure boxes of our day. Will we engage these ancient practices and allow the Holy Spirit to teach us through them? Or will we just throw them away?

I'll take revelation over relevance any day.

I collect antiques. One of my favorite pieces I have is a Victor Gramophone. It's old, and it doesn't really work well. But there is something about it that draws me. The inner workings of this old record player are so intricate, so well designed, and so beautiful. I love the way the brass horn distorts the sound of the vinyl record. There is a different sound that comes out of this antique that can't be replicated by my iPhone and Bluetooth speaker.

I love the Desert Fathers [1] for this reason! These people spent lifetimes in prayer and solitude. The early monastics have practices that are antique in their nature, but there is no other way to replicate their sound.

At first, I didn't understand the relevancy of Song of Solomon.

Then, after I began reading, the Holy Spirit began breathing. Song of Solomon had me spinning! If I could find out how much Jesus loves the Church through this love story written by King Solomon, perhaps I can find more hidden gems in the life of King Solomon as recorded in the historical books.

In Romans 16, Paul closes his epistle with a doxology. In this doxology he addresses the hidden secrets of the Old Testament writings.

"Now to him who is able to strengthen you according to my gospel and the preaching of Jesus Christ, according to the revelation of the mystery that was kept secret for long ages but has now been disclosed and through the prophetic writings has been made known to all nations, according to the command of the

eternal God, to bring about the obedience of faith— to the only wise God be glory forevermore through Jesus Christ! Amen." [2]

Romans 16:15-17 ESV

God has been writing the Gospel since the very beginning! All scriptures point to Jesus! This is great news! There is such a depth of wisdom available to us in the Old Testament. If we kneel before the Holy Spirit with the books of the Old Testament, he will reveal Jesus.

I began my search.

I found an interesting story in 1 Kings 2:13-22.

So walk with me as we read about Jesus through the life of King Solomon.

Solomon is appointed king. However, Solomon is not a single child. He had many brothers who each wanted the throne. Adonijah was

I'M AFRAID WE OFTEN TOSS OUT THINGS THAT WE DON'T BELIEVE TO BE RELEVANT TO US. IN DOING SO, WE MAY THROW OUT A HIDDEN MESSAGE THE HOLY SPIRIT IS PATIENTLY WAITING TO BREATHE ON.

one of Solomon's brothers who seemed to be the most interested in his crowned destiny. He felt he deserved to be made king instead of Solomon. He felt robbed. So, he went to Solomon's mother Bathsheba and made a request. He knew that Solomon wouldn't deny a request from his own mother. Adonijah asked for Abishag, Solomon's beloved. Now, Solomon had quite a few wives... seven hundred to be precise.

Abishag was different.

She wasn't a diplomatic marriage.

She wasn't arranged to marry him.

Solomon chose her.

He had never seen a girl more beautiful.

He was head over heels for her.

He loved her.

Abishag was Solomon's favorite.

She was the subject of Song of Solomon.

Adonijah knew that she was his brother's bride. He reasoned, "Solomon got the whole kingdom, the least I'm asking for is one girl." Perhaps he was thinking, I could still take a jab at my brother so he isn't entirely happy. You know how brothers are... If I can't have everything that I want, then neither can they! Another reason scholars believe Adonijah asked for Abishag was to lay a claim to the throne himself. Why Bathsheba wanted to help Adonijah is beside me. Maybe she was being a good mom and trying to make peace between the feuding siblings. Regardless, Bathsheba presents the request to the new king.

Solomon's response blew me away. It reminded me of Jesus's love for the Church – you and me.

Solomon was shocked that Adonijah would even ask for his bride. He said, "Why would he ask for Abishag? He might as well have asked for the whole kingdom. It's more likely that I'd give him that!"

What a love! Solomon would have rather given up the kingdom than his beloved.

It's the same attitude Jesus has for us.

"Think of yourselves the way Christ Jesus thought of himself. He had equal status with God but didn't think so much of himself that he had to cling to the advantages of that status no matter what. Not at all. When the time came, he set aside the privileges of deity and took on the status of a slave, became human! Having become human, he stayed human. It was an incredibly humbling process. He didn't claim special privileges. Instead, he lived a selfless, obedient life and then died a selfless, obedient death— and the worst kind of death at that—a crucifixion." [3]

Philippians 2:5-8 MSG

Jesus didn't only say he was willing to give up everything for us, HE DID!

Jesus actually left Heaven and came to earth. He gave up his status and rank and humbled himself. He went after his bride.

Jesus gave everything he had for us. He loves us so much that he denied every right he had and took on all the sin that was rightfully ours.

What a deep love!

If we want to have a Christ-like love for others, we need to be willing to give up everything.

Just like Jesus did.

I've done my fair share of traveling.

One of my favorite trips I've ever taken was to Germany.

I went to Germany for a very important reason. Each year, a group of missionaries from undisclosed nations around the world meet to have a retreat. These families are some of, if not the only Christians in their nations. They live among people who do not understand them, are scared and skeptical of them, and potentially hostile toward them. During this week, my team and I put on a kid's camp for the kids and students. We have games, and dramas, and object lessons. We have candy, and videos, and bonfires! It is a really special week. These families are superheroes. Though none of them would say it.

They have all fallen in love with a nation. And just like Jesus, they have given up all the benefits of their status and wealth to go after the ones they love.

I have seen, year after year, these missionaries painstakingly learn their nation's language, culture, nuances, customs, cuisines, and more. They have given up more than most. All for love. Many of them never see a mass revival. Instead, they rejoice in one soul saved. They tell the story of casually befriending a neighbor and eventually leading them to the Lord like they are recounting playing in the Super Bowl. In my opinion, a soul saved is a much bigger deal!

In the American church, we often forget about the importance of sacrifice.

We get so comfortable living in our privilege that we become blind to what is truly important. We love ourselves too much. Many of us don't even know what it's like to love someone else enough to sacrifice everything for them. We are self-preserving while Jesus sets the example of self-sacrifice.

We are comfortable, while Jesus was uncomfortable. We are selfish, while Jesus is selfless.

When I interact with people like my friends abroad, I feel convicted. I start to notice all the areas in my life where I have compromised for comfort.

Maybe you're feeling a little bit of conviction right now.

Time isn't up. You can still give it all. You can still be like Jesus and fall in love with the very people Jesus died for.

Maybe you aren't ready to give everything away. Maybe you aren't supposed to. Jesus will ask you for what you have when it is the right time. The question isn't, are you ready to give it all? The question is, are you willing to give it all?

What if he asks for your job?

Your home?

Your car?

Your shoes?

Your voice?

I know it's easy to say you will give it all up when the time comes.

But will you really?

I had just left my very first pastoral position. I was getting paid well.

I loved the families. I loved the church. But God was calling me else-where. I didn't know where. I just knew it was time to go. So I went. God called me to give up security and a salary in exchange for a lot of unanswered questions.

I went on a three-month missions trip and then came back to unemployment.

I still had no idea what I was going to do. All I knew was that God had called me to student ministry in Michigan. I spent the summer living with my parents and waiting.

To pass the time, and because it's my favorite thing to do in the whole wide world, I went to church camp. At the camp, the speaker took an offering for Speed The Light, a missionary partnership organization. They buy cars and motorcycles, sound systems, and donkeys for mis-sionaries all over the globe. The students got on board with the vision of giving more than we had ever given in a single week at camp. It was awesome to see everyone's excitement.

I was standing in the back of the auditorium as the students gave their offerings. Keep in mind, I hadn't had a job for the past six months and I had no prospects on the horizon. Giving to the Speed The Light of-fering was the last thing on my mind. So I observed.

Until the speaker grabbed the microphone and said, "I believe God is laying it on leader's and youth pastor's hearts to personally give a thousand dollars this week."

"Nope. Not me" I thought.

But the Lord said, "Yes, you."

I rationalized how fiscally irresponsible it would be for me to give that much money. I didn't know how long I would be without a job. I had expenses I had to take care of. So, I took a deep breath and started thinking of literally anything else.

The moment came and went. I felt fine. No deep conviction. No butterflies in my stomach. Nothing. All good.

That is... until the next day.

In the morning, the service was entirely dedicated to Speed The Light. The second I heard "STL" my heart sank. Immediately a million steel butterflies manifested in my gut and flapped their wings as hard as they could. I heard the Lord say,

"Give."

There was no denying it. But I wasn't going to give a thousand dollars without a fight. So, I kept resisting.

James 4:7 says, **"Resist the devil and he will flee from you."** [4]

The problem was, I wasn't resisting the devil... I was resisting God.

God didn't flee. He never does.

The daunting thought wouldn't leave my mind, which just proved more and more that it was God.

I ran to my car and grabbed my checkbook. When I came back, it was too late. They had already announced the final tally. It was just over $16,000.

I grabbed the guy in charge and told him that I was fighting it, but I wanted to raise the total to an even $17,000. He knew I didn't have a job and looked at me with a puzzled face. When I gave him the check, he whispered, "Do you even have that much?"

I was a bit embarrassed. I didn't want his pity. I confirmed that the check wouldn't bounce. He ran up to the stage and told the speaker the updated total.

The speaker was visibly excited!

What I didn't know was earlier in the week he had been praying for the camp. The Lord told him that we would give $17,000 to Speed The Light that week. He told the leader of the camp, who confirmed the story.

We didn't just celebrate the record-breaking offering for our camp.
We celebrated the obedience of every single person who gave.
My story is just one of many.

How many students submitted to God's call to give $20 or even $100?

How many other leaders could empathize with my experience?

The total didn't just represent dollars. It represented the obedience of people who sacrificed for love.

Just like Jesus.

It is so easy to get trapped in a self-serving mindset.

We do what we can to benefit our own life. We work to pay our bills

We give toward our pleasures. In a hyper pleasure seeking culture, it is difficult to learn how to be selfless.

It is completely counter cultural.

Francis Chan addresses this issue in his incredible book, Letters to The Church.

"Many of us make decisions based on what brings us the most pleasure, This is how we choose our homes, jobs, cars, clothes, food, and churches. We pursue what we want; then we make sure there are no biblical commands we are violating. In essence, we want to know what God will tolerate rather than what he desires. Ignorance feels better than disobedience." [5]

Letters to The Church, pp. 53-54

Have Western Christians become so indoctrinated by a consumerism culture that we are incapable of imitating Jesus' supernatural selflessness?

It's a scary thought to entertain.

I am afraid Western Christianity has inadvertently begun worshiping an idol much more dangerous than Molech, Asherah, or even Baal. We have sacrificed our finances, our time, our talents, and even the wellbeing of others, to a false triune god affectionately known as "Me, Myself, and I".

The idol of our own self interest has stolen the worship that rightfully belongs to Yahweh.

We have created a religion around supporting our own interests and worldly desires. Instead of self-denial, we promote self-indulgence. Instead of suffering we promote pleasure. Instead of giving, we promote gaining.

Greg Boyd, in his book The Myth of a Christian Religion calls this concept "MeChurch".

"MeChurch not only fails to confront the idols and pagan values of Western culture, it often "Christianizes" them. Not only do we not have to give up our possessions, as Jesus commands; we're told that following Jesus ensures that we'll get more of them!" [6]

The Myth of a Christian Nation, pp. 77

Is there any hope?

Of course there is!

Our hope is found in Jesus.

When we look at Jesus, we see what a worthy and beautiful God we imitate.

The question is, how do we see Jesus?

Each and every one of us "Jesus People" are his reflection. As we imitate Jesus and show the world what selflessness looks like, others jump on board.

I grew up in an environment that shared missionary stories week after week in church. I read books about missionaries. I watched movies about missionaries. Missionaries were my heroes when I was growing up; and they still are today!

When we live a self-sacrificial life like Jesus, not seeking our own interests but the needs of others, people take notice.

Selflessness is the match that ignites the dry heart of a person on the cusp of really, truly, following Jesus.

The Western Church has compromised itself. There is no getting past this simple and sad truth. However, the Western Church has not fallen outside the reach of Jesus.

I believe as Christians begin to practice the spiritual discipline of self-denial, the Church in the West will begin to ignite! A movement is stirring. A revolution is on the verge of breaking out. Selfless Jesus People are rising up and sacrificing the desires of the world for the desires of God.

There is a bright future for the Church as people sacrifice for the sake of love, just like Jesus.

INTERMISSION

AS I MENTIONED IN CHAPTER 3, I AM A THEATER KID.

SO, IT SEEMS FITTING TO HAVE A BRIEF INTERMISSION.

"BE LIKE JESUS" IS NOT A PASSIVE ENCOURAGEMENT BY ANY MEANS. IT'S A CHARGE TO ENGAGE AND PARTICIPATE IN THE WAY OF JESUS. IT'S EASY TO READ A BOOK AND BE ENCOURAGED WITH A GOOD IDEA. AND LET'S FACE IT "BE LIKE JESUS" IS 100% THE BEST IDEA YOU'VE EVER HEARD. I DONT TAKE THE CREDIT FOR COMING UP WITH IT EITHER. IT'S THE BEST IDEA EVER. IT'S JESUS' IDEA. I'M JUST A MESSENGER.

IT IS A VERY DIFFERENT THING HOWEVER, TO ACTUALLY BEGIN RESTRUCTURING OUR LIVES TO CONFORM TO THE LIFESTYLE OF JESUS. THAT'S THE PURPOSE OF THIS INTERMISSION.

WHAT I WANT TO ENCOURAGE YOU TO DO IN THESE NEXT FEW PAGES, IS TO PRACTICALLY TAKE STEPS TO STRATEGICALLY LIVE LIKE JESUS.

FOLLOW WHAT I LIKE TO CALL, THE ABC'S OF PERSONAL ACCOUNTABILITY.

ASK THE HOLY SPIRIT TO SHOW YOU PLACES IN YOUR LIFE WHERE YOU CAN IMPROVE IN YOUR EFFORTS TO BE LIKE JESUS.

BE HONEST WITH YOURSELF.

COMMIT TO THE DISCIPLINES YOU DEVELOP.

DO WHAT YOU SET OUT TO DO!

FILL OUT THE FOLLOWING WEEKLY CALENDAR WITH YOUR IDEAL WEEK. LIST THINGS YOU WISH TO ACCOMPLISH, TIME YOU WOULD LIKE TO SET ASIDE TO SPEND WITH THE LORD, YOUR FAMILY, STUDIES, AND HOBBIES.

SUNDAY
Church/ Time with fam

MONDAY
Fun day

TUESDAY
Relax

WEDNESDAY
Relax

THURSDAY
Hondea
Hang with Seth's fam

FRIDAY
Hair Apt.

SATURDAY
Sabbath / Family day

OVER THE NEXT WEEK, TRACK YOUR PROGRESS. DID YOU DO WHAT YOU THOUGHT YOU WOULD DO? DID YOU DO BETTER THAN YOU EXPECTED? OR DID YOU FALL SHORT OF YOUR GOAL? HOW CAN YOU RESTRUCTURE YOUR DAY TO BE LESS FULL OF HURRY AND MORE FULL OF THINGS THAT BRING LIFE TO YOUR SOUL AND THOSE AROUND YOU?

WHAT ARE TWO ATTRIBUTES OF JESUS' CHARACTER THAT YOU CAN INTENTIONALLY IMITATE IN THE COMING MONTH?

- REMEMBER IT TAKES ABOUT A MONTH OF REPETITION TO FORM A NEW HABIT -

- Never being in a rush
- Trusting in Gods plan

WHO CAN YOU ENCOURAGE THIS WEEK? LIST SEVEN PEOPLE YOU CAN TAKE TIME TO PRAY FOR AND REACH OUT TO EACH DAY. MAKE IT A PRIORITY TO SHARE AN ENCOURAGING WORD WITH THEM.

TELL THEM WHAT YOU WERE PRAYING OVER THEM. SHARE ANY WORD THE LORD SHARED WITH YOU REGARDING THEIR LIFE.

1. Promise
2. Doreen
3. Naz
4. Marriisa
5. Bayli
6. Rose
7. Hanna

OFTENTIMES IN THE GOSPELS, JESUS WAS LED BY COMPASSION.

IF JESUS WERE TO SPEND A DAY IN YOUR SHOES, WHERE WOULD HIS COMPASSION TAKE HIM?

WHAT WOULD HE DO WHEN HE GOT WHERE HE WAS GOING? WOULD JESUS BE LED TO THE NEARBY HOMELESS SHELTER TO CARE FOR THOSE IN NEED? WOULD JESUS BE LED TO THE ASSISTED LIVING HOME TO SING SONGS TO THE ELDERLY? WOULD JESUS BE LED TO THE PUBLIC SCHOOLS TO DONATE SCHOOL SUPPLIES TO CHILDREN WHO NEED A HELPING HAND?

IDENTIFY AN AREA OF YOUR WORLD YOU CAN INFLUENCE AS AN IMITATOR OF CHRIST.

- Youth Students
- College Students

IT TAKES A DETERMINATION TO CONFORM YOUR LIFE TO THE LIFESTYLE OF CHRIST.
AND THAT CAN'T HAPPEN ALONE.

NAME 3 PEOPLE YOU CAN CONNECT WITH AND SHARE YOUR PROCESS WITH.

ASK THEM TO HOLD YOU ACCOUNTABLE TO THE THINGS YOU SET OUT TO DO.
BE OPEN WITH THEM AND ASK THEM TO ENCOURAGE YOU IN YOUR PERSONAL
JOURNEY TO BE LIKE JESUS.

1 _Seth_____

2 _Naz_____

3 _Doreen_____

HONESTLY, IF YOU DILIGENTLY SEEK TO BE LIKE JESUS, YOU WILL WITHOUT A DOUBT BECOME LIKE JESUS.

JESUS IS CONSTANTLY BECKONING US TO IMITATE HIM. WE JUST NEED TO ACCEPT THE INVITATION. WE ACCEPT THE INVITATION BY PRACTICING THE WAY OF JESUS. AS WE PRACTICE THE WAY, WE ALLOW THE HOLY SPIRIT TO TRANSFORM US INTO THE LIKENESS OF CHRIST. PRACTICING THE WAY OF JESUS IS OUR CONTRACT WITH THE LORD, WE AGREE TO BE CONFORMED TO HIS IMAGE. AS WE PRACTICE THE CHARACTER OF CHRIST, OUR VERY NATURE IS REPROGRAMMED. UNTIL, WE ARE NO LONGER PRACTICING. WE ARE LIVING AS NEW CREATIONS WHO LIVE LIKE JESUS.

DALLAS WILLARD HAS THIS TO SAY ABOUT THE PROCESS OF BECOMING LIKE JESUS.

"JESUS NEVER EXPECTED US SIMPLY TO TURN THE OTHER CHEEK, GO THE SECOND MILE, BLESS THOSE WHO PERSECUTE US, GIVE UNTO THEM THAT ASK, AND SO FORTH. THESE RESPONSES, GENERALLY AND RIGHTLY UNDERSTOOD TO BE CHARACTERISTIC OF CHRISTLIKENESS, WERE SET FORTH BY HIM AS ILLUSTRATIVE OF WHAT MIGHT BE EXPECTED OF A NEW KIND OF PERSON — ONE WHO INTELLIGENTLY AND STEADFASTLY SEEKS, ABOVE ALL ELSE, TO LIVE WITHIN THE RULE OF GOD AND BE POSSESSED BY THE KIND OF RIGHTEOUSNESS THAT GOD HIMSELF HAS, AS MATTHEW 6:33 PORTRAYS. INSTEAD, JESUS DID INVITE PEOPLE TO FOLLOW HIM INTO THAT SORT OF LIFE FROM WHICH BEHAVIOR SUCH AS LOVING ONE'S ENEMIES WILL SEEM LIKE THE ONLY SENSIBLE AND HAPPY THING TO DO. FOR A PERSON LIVING THAT LIFE, THE HARD THING TO DO WOULD BE TO HATE THE ENEMY, TO TURN THE SUPPLICANT AWAY, OR TO CURSE THE CURSER... TRUE CHRISTLIKENESS, TRUE COMPANIONSHIP WITH CHRIST, COMES AT THE POINT WHERE IT IS HARD NOT TO RESPOND AS HE WOULD." [1]

SO GOOD! WE HAVE A HOPE THAT WE WILL NOT ONLY BE LIKE JESUS IN THE HEREAFTER, BUT WE WILL BE LIKE JESUS IN THE HERE AND NOW! AMEN!

THE LIGHTS ARE FLASHING.

WHICH MEANS THE INTERMISSION HAS COME TO AN END.

PLEASE ENJOY THE REST OF THE SHOW...

I MEAN, BOOK.

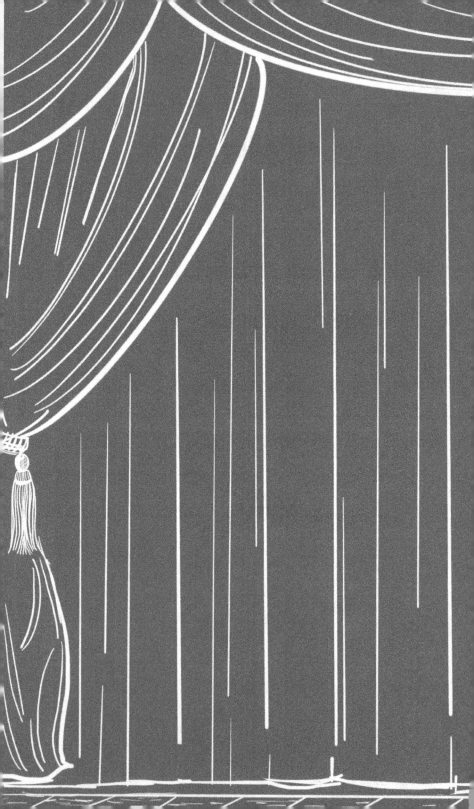

HOT ROCK
HONOR
POPSICLES

GOOD LEADERS KNOW HOW TO GOOF AROUND

CHAPTER 8

GOOD LEADERS KNOW HOW TO GOOF AROUND

There is a small basketball training camp in southeast Michigan.

You'll find it at the beginning of June, in Gary's back yard. Around two to three hundred students gather on this property every summer.

The camp is invitation only.

It is free.

It is fun.

It's special.

A group of a few dozen coaches make up the camp's staff. These coaches come from all over the world to volunteer their time and take part in this week of ministry to student athletes. Why?

That's easy.

Gary.

Gary is a physical therapist. Many would refer to him as the father of modern physical therapy. He has invented and developed systems, recovery tracks, and equipment to help people heal. As he would tell you, "God does the healing. I provide the place for it to happen." Gary has helped provide that healing atmosphere to many of the greatest athletes in history. You know the names of the athletes, but you don't know the name of the physical therapist that helped them get back into the game after an injury. Gary prefers it that way. He is a truly humble man; by anyone's standards. Gary invites three hundred kids into his backyard every summer to ruin his grass, rather than sit in his trophy room and boast about his worldly accomplishments.

There is a secret about Hot Rock.

I'm not sure that many people know the truth about this one-of-a-kind camp.

Hot Rock is not a basketball camp.

Sure there are about a thousand basketballs, three full courts, and a dozen hoops in Gary's yard.

Something is hidden.

What you don't see is the very kingdom of Heaven. It's invisible to the naked eye. But, when you are a part of the camp, it's like a veil is lifted. You realize Gary doesn't open his home to a basketball camp each year so kids can become better athletes. He opens his home to Heaven so kids can experience real life, real joy, and real love through a real God.

Each and every year they do. There is never an altar call. There is never an offering. There is never an alter call where a pianist softly plays *Waymaker* in the background.

There are basketballs.

There is a slip n' slide.

There are a lot of popsicles.

Most importantly, there is a group of honorable men and women who have one objective in mind, to love and serve the hundreds of young men who attend the camp.

Gary doesn't dim the lights, play soft worship music, and fill a room with smoke to help people to encounter God. He plays basketball with them and invites his friends to play too. The agenda is fun. And when kids have fun, they experience God, because God created fun. God created this beautiful world and it's his desire that we enjoy the life he created.

Each and every year when I step on Gary's property I am welcomed by a community of authentic, humble, and loving men of faith. Are any of us perfect? Honestly, if you asked that question in a coach's breakfast/team huddle, you'd get a resounding laugh along with a firm "hell no!"

Which speaks for itself.

Gary likes to goof around and encourages the coaches and campers to do the same. I've seen young campers rub bomb pops on Gary's bald head, splash ice water on their coaches, and attack the cameraman.

> **HONOR LOOKS LIKE A MELTED POPSICLE RUNNING DOWN YOUR FACE AND FIVE SMILING LITTLE KIDS LAUGHING BEHIND YOU MORE THAN IT LOOKS LIKE PEOPLE FOLLOWING YOUR ORDERS.**

At Hot Rock, respect is important... but so is fun.

We goof around every day for an entire week, all while getting coached and educated by some of the best and brightest minds in athletics.

This camp's atmosphere is literally unlike anywhere I've ever been.

It's different.

It's holy.

I feel Heaven at Hot Rock.

Goofing around and respect should coincide. It's a paradox. Goofing around often looks disrespectful, like how when I was a camper, we used to pants Doug (Gary's son and director of Hot Rock). Respect often looks unfunny, like listening intently to your coach during a pre-game speech. But respect and goofing around exist together in harmony in Gary's backyard.

The only way respect and goofing around can exist together is through humility.

In Romans 12:3, Paul instructs us to not take ourselves to seriously.

Be confidant in who you are.

Take a joke.

Laugh a little.

You're not that important.

If Gary can sit in a chair while kids melt popsicles on his head, you can too.

In our morning huddles, Gary reminds us to goof around. The camp doesn't work if we don't. The same is true for life. If we take everything too seriously, we forget about our mortality. We forget that we only have a short amount of time to participate in this life God created for us.

Gaining the respect of others is important, but if there is one thing I've learned while watching Gary, it is that respect follows closely behind humility.

Proverbs 29:23 says, **"One's pride will bring him low, but he who is lowly in spirit will obtain honor."** [1]

Pride says, "I deserve respect."

Humility believes the opposite. Humility understands that apart from God, we truly have nothing. Humility understands that the ten talents in your hand are a gift. Humility breaths each borrowed breath with appreciation. Pride feels entitled to honor and moans when it does not receive it.

Pride shouts, "I earned this with my own blood, sweat, and tears!"

Humility knows that the only blood, sweat, and tears that truly matter belong to Jesus.

How can we look in the face of Jesus and think we deserve anything? How can we stand at the foot of the cross and believe we are deserving of respect? How audacious is it of us that we use the very breath God gifted us to demand people submit to our every whim?

How could we?

Lord, forgive us.

Honor looks like a melted Popsicle running down your face and five smiling little kids laughing behind you more than it looks like people following your orders.

In ministry, I have gotten to know many truly humble people.

I have also gotten to know some prideful people.

I could tell a few horror stories here, but I won't. I don't need to. I'm sure you have interacted with your fair share of arrogant people in your lifetime. Maybe you, like me, were once one of those arrogant people. I used to think respect was earned. I used to think I was entitled to honor because of what I had done.

I couldn't have been more wrong.

Honor is not something you can attain. It is not something to be had. Honor is a perception one person has for another based on the humility he or she exemplifies.

People don't honor tyrants; they fear them. Take away the power, take away the threat, and take away the pomp and status – do people still follow? If they do, that's true honor. Humility is a hidden treasure.

It's hard to find, but well worth the search.

To serve someone who is truly humble is a beautiful thing. It is liberating, enjoyable, and honoring both to the follower and the leader.

Gary enjoys leading this camp. I enjoy following his leadership.

He has never ordered me to do anything. Instead, he has thanked me for being present. He is constantly telling me how glad he is that I am at Hot Rock. He doesn't tell me what a privilege it is for me to be there. He doesn't throw his credibility in my face and demand I respect him. Instead, he genuinely feels honored that I would spend the week in his backyard.

Yeah, that's right. He feels honored that "I" would spend the week playing Noce Ball [2] "his" backyard.

People who are truly honorable don't remind you why they deserve it. People who demand respect will never get it. They may get their employees and subordinates to follow their orders, but they will never have their hearts.

Honor comes from the heart.

———

Jesus was qualified. He was not only a brilliant intellectual. He was considered a prophet and teacher. He was also a skilled tradesman.

He was a killer fisherman too, by the way.

Jesus was deserving of respect from every earthly standard. Not to mention his divinity! There is no one more deserving of honor than Jesus. Yet, even Jesus, in his humility, considered others of more importance than himself.

He came to serve.

The world believes that honor is something to be earned through authoritative means, but Jesus teaches a backwards way of thinking. It's counter cultural.

You should want to serve.

You should not seek to become great.

It is better to give than to receive.

In Mark 10 we see a story unfold that depicts this paradox perfectly.

James and John feel a special bond with Jesus. They believed that

Jesus would soon be established on his throne. I believe their under-standing was that Jesus would be established as the earthly king of Israel. Could they have been referring to Heaven? Perhaps, but judg-ing by the misguided motives, I would think it is more probable they were referring to an earthly reign.

In this forecast regime, they wanted to be part of the action.

They came to Jesus and asked if they could sit next to him when he is on his throne, one at the right and one to the left of him. Jesus didn't skip a beat when he rhetorically asked them, "You want to sit on a throne?"

They nodded their heads.

Jesus subtly laughed to himself, "Well, do you want to do what I'm about to do? Will you also suffer and die?"

They nodded once again.

"Well then. You will."

James and John got excited. What they thought they heard was, "[You will] surly sit at my side on a nice comfy throne." What Jesus actually said was, "[You will] surely suffer like I do."

Upon realizing the interpretive error, their faces sobered up.

"But to sit at my side is not for me to choose. You can't buy yourself a seat at the table. It's a gift of grace."

The other disciples became angry that James and John would even ask such a thing.

Perhaps a few of them were angry they didn't think to ask the question earlier.Jesus calmed them down and then taught…

"You know that those who are considered rulers of the Gentiles lord it over them, and their great ones exercise authority over them. But it shall not be so among you. But whoever would be great among you must be your servant, and whoever would be first among you must be slave of all. For even the Son of Man came not to be served but to serve, and to give his life as a ransom for many." [3]

Mark 10:42-45 ESV

Jesus points out how the rulers in power demand respect. They believe they are entitled to honor. Jesus said that's not how his kingdom will work. His kingdom will be one of true honor and humility.

The Message paraphrase makes this passage much easier to understand.

When the other ten heard of this conversation, they lost their tempers with James and John. Jesus got them together to settle things down. "You've observed how godless rulers throw their weight around," he said, "and when people get a little power how quickly it goes to their heads. It's not going to be that way with you. Whoever wants to be great must become a servant. Whoever wants to be first among you must be your slave. That is what the Son of Man has done: He came to serve, not to be served— and then to give away his life in exchange for many who are held hostage." [4]

Mark 10:41-45 MSG

Jesus teaches us that humility leads to true honor.

He not only teaches it, he lives it out.

In another story in John 13 we see a specific moment Jesus led by example.

"When he had washed their feet and put on his outer garments and resumed his place, he said to them, "Do you understand what I have done to you? You call me teacher and Lord, and you are right, for so I am. If I then, your Lord and teacher, have washed your feet, you also ought to wash one another's feet. For I have given you an example, that you also should do just as I have done to you. Truly, truly, I say to you, a servant is not greater than his master, nor is a messenger greater than the one who sent him. If you know these things, blessed are you if you do them." [5]

John 13:12-17 ESV

Could it be any clearer?

If Jesus considered himself a servant, if he washed the disciples' feet, how could we continue to demand honor from another? Jesus set the example. Don't live a life where you feel entitled to praise. None but Jesus is deserving of praise.

Don't demand respect from those around you; instead, give it.

Serve and put others ahead of yourself.

Goof around and let kids melt popsicles on your head.

Pass honor around like hot potato; or maybe more appropriately, a Hot Rock.

SUBMISSION

MOMS

BLUE+YELLOW

PRACTICE RECIPROCAL SUBMISSION

CHAPTER 9

PRACTICE RECIPROCAL SUBMISSION

Jesus and his first disciples were attending a wedding at a place called Cana. The night seemed to be going off without a hitch. Everyone was enjoying themselves... maybe a little too much. The reception wasn't even over and they had already finished the wine.

The party was at a standstill. Nobody knew what to do. The night was coming to an early end. Mary, Jesus' mother, noticed that people were getting a little antsy as she overheard certain guests planning to leave the wedding early. Concerned for the bride and groom, and the dignity of the wedding, she knew she needed to come up with a solution for the lack of wine.

She knew exactly who to talk to.

How did she know Jesus could solve this problem? Had he done this kind of thing before? Did Mary know something no one else knew? Nevertheless, she ran to her son.

"Jesus!" She said as she inserted herself into the circle of disciples surrounding him. "They don't have anymore wine."

"That's not my problem." Jesus went back to his conversation.

But Mary stood staring at Jesus with a look only a mother could give. Jesus couldn't ignore his mom.

A bit annoyed, he reacted, "It's not time."

Jesus raised his eyebrows and his eyes got big as he tried to nonverbally communicate to his mom something no one else could know.

"I'm not planning on doing any miracles now. I need to lay low a little longer."

He whispered the secret message to his mother.

She didn't seem to be as concerned with his cover as he was. Mary instead turned to the servants at the party. "You two... come here." She instructed with sternness only a woman planning a wedding could muster. "Do whatever he tells you to do."

"Now there were six stone water jars there for the Jewish rites of purification, each holding twenty or thirty gallons. Jesus said to the servants, "Fill the jars with water." And they filled them up to the brim. And he said to them, "Now draw some out and take it to the master of the feast." So they took it. When the master of the feast tasted the water now become wine, and did not know where it came from (though the servants who had drawn the water knew), the master of the feast called the bridegroom and said to him, "Everyone serves the good wine first, and when people have drunk freely, then the poor wine. But you have kept the good wine until now." This, the first of his signs, Jesus did at Cana in Galilee, and manifested his glory. And his disciples believed in him." [1]

John 2:6-11 ESV

My mom was a youth leader.

She loves ministering to students.

That's where I get it from. I remember growing up as a kid in the youth group. I would get to attend youth events that no other kids my age could attend. It was the best childhood someone could ask for. My mom is great at being a youth leader. I remember when I first became a pastor, she cautioned me to remember the leaders. She explained a very simple concept that was in many ways contradictory to the leadership instruction I had been taught by others.

"Never forget that the leaders you have under you can do exactly what you are doing. They have good ideas too."

This leadership perspective was developed over decades of volunteer youth leadership experience. It made sense in theory.

"Of course." I thought. "I would never think of my volunteers as less than me."

But, keeping this philosophy became more difficult than I had anticipated. It is easy to get your way when you are in charge. It is difficult to submit to your subordinates.

There is the issue.

In life, we have no subordinates.

We have partners.

We have brothers.

We have sisters.

We have co-laborers in Christ.

SUBMISSION IS LIKE ANY SACRIFICE. IT REQUIRES YOU TO GIVE UP SOME- THING, (YOUR OWN WAY OF DOING SOMETHING) TO SOMEONE ELSE.

The Apostle Paul doesn't write his epistles to his "Loyal Followers" or "Faithful Volunteers".

He addresses the people in the churches as his friends, brothers and sisters, and co-laborers.

This is vital!

As people in positions of authority, we must strive all the more to be humble and consider others as more important than ourselves.

Paul says in Philippians 2:3-4, **"Do nothing from selfish ambition or conceit, but in humility count others more significant than yourselves. Let each of you look not only to his own interests, but also to the interests of others."** [2]

The word used for "others" in verse 3 is allelon, which implies, reciprocity. We not only consider others more significant, it's a mutual understanding that every member of the group should have.

When people are reciprocating support and encouragement, wouldn't you know it, everyone gets support and encouragement.

Think for a second of a group standing in a circle. Each individual in the circle is holding a pie.

I do love pie. Any chance I get to use pie in an illustration, you better believe I'll do it!

I was living with my friend and his family during the Covid-19 stay at home order. He is an excellent pie maker. We participated in a challenge called 30 Days, 30 Pies. It was one of the most amazing things I've ever experienced. Talk about making the most of the quarentine!

I digress. Back to the illustration! I highly encourage you try this little experiment at home.

Each person in the circle chooses one person in the circle to give their pie to. They count down from three and deliver their pies. In this system, the pies will be unevenly distributed. Certain people will get more pies than others. Certain people will not get any pie. Now, substitute pie for encouragement and support. When we choose who gets encouragement and support based on an arbitrary set of classifications, we exclude certain members of our group.

This is what I see at work in the current church hierarchical leadership structure. It's not a bad thing. Hierarchies are good. They are natural. They promote innovation and competition. They spur good ideas and fresh solutions to old problems. However, in the kingdom, hierarchies work down and around, not up.

Oftentimes, the system of leadership becomes unbalanced, we have a few people at the top gaining all the appreciation and a few at the bottom who go unnoticed.

There is another way we often distribute the pies. Imagine each person in the circle eats their own pie.

Sure, everyone gets pie. But, nobody gets the joy that comes with giving or receiving. It's one thing to buy yourself a gift, it is another thing to receive exactly what you want from someone who cares about you. And it's even better to watch someone's face light up as they open the gift you gave them!

The selfish, individualist approach doesn't work either.

Now, imagine each member in the circle passes a pie to the person next to them. They consider the person next to them as the most important person in the world! They pass pies around and around the circle. Because, there is always someone next to them, there is always someone to pass the pie to. They share around and around!

Everyone gives.

Everyone receives.

All are supported.

All are encouraged.

All are selflessly giving to each other!

And everyone gets pie!

This is the leadership system Jesus institutes. The person next to you is the most important person in the world. When we are all considering the person next to us to be the most important person in the world, we are united!

As the Psalmist says in Psalms 133:1, **"Behold, how good and pleasant it is when brothers dwell in unity!"** [3] It is good and pleasant because everyone gets what they need and everyone is able to participate in giving.

I've heard leaders preach about the importance of unity. They demand the people under their authority to unify their hearts to the leader's vision. But, as leaders, we need to take a step down and unify ourselves with the vision of the people and submit ourselves to what God is doing in the church.

Everything in the kingdom is upside down; including the role of a leader. As leaders, we need to understand that submission is a two-way street. Paul writes this instruction in Ephesians 5.

"**Look carefully then how you walk, not as unwise but as wise, making the best use of the time, because the days are evil. Therefore do not be foolish, but understand what the will of the Lord is. And do not get drunk with wine, for that is debauchery, but be filled with the Spirit, addressing one another in psalms and hymns and spiritual songs, singing and making melody to the Lord with your heart, giving thanks always and for everything to God the Father in the name of our Lord Jesus Christ, submitting to one another out of reverence for Christ.** [4]

Ephesians 5:15-21 ESV

Submission must always be reciprocal.

We need to make sure there is a good balance in our lives. If you notice you get your way most of the time, make a change. Your ideas are probably awesome. Seriously, they are! But you're not the only one with awesome ideas.

Submission is like any sacrifice. It requires you to give up something, (your own way of doing something) to someone else. Ultimately, when we submit to one another, we are submitting to God. We are figuratively saying to God, "Lord, I will not make an idol of my way."

It is hard to give up your way of doing things, but when we do, the church grows.

The result of reciprocal submission is unity and trust.

It goes without saying that as a leader, you will need to make decisions not everyone agrees with or benefits from. These decisions are hard and must be handled with grace and patience. Tearing off the Band Aid works in fewer scenarios than your lack of patience would lead you to believe. Don't rush leadership.

A pastor friend of mine shared with me a vision he had after taking over as lead pastor of his church. He said he was on a big sailboat. The boat was going in the wrong direction and needed to turn. He could throw the wheel viciously in one direction and send the boat into an immediate about-face. But in doing that, he would risk people losing their balance and falling overboard. So, knowing he had to make a complete 180-degree turn, he turned slowly.

Keeping the boat level became his first priority. Getting to where they needed to go came second. As leaders, no matter what you lead, God has given you vision and direction. It's easy to run full speed after those dreams. But running too far ahead leaves people behind.

It's hard to be a servant to those you either threw off the boat, or left in your dust.

When people feel like they never get their way, they either leave or rebel.

Reciprocal submission sets the standard of mutual trust and appreciation and ultimately, unity. When people know they can trust you, they will go the extra mile.

I was a greenhorn in Northville, Michigan, in my first pastoral position. I was intent on not screwing it up. I would email my volunteer team with all of their responsibilities and assignments. I would have a flowchart and my sermon notes typed up.

We called it a flowchart because in kid's ministry, though it is good to have structure, you better be ready to go with the flow!

Bethann was one of our kid's leaders. She was also the director of

Royal Family Kids Camp. [5] RFK is a wonderful organization that provides a camp experience to kids in foster care amongst other things. One of her many responsibilities at this camp is to lead a team of high school students to put on a drama for the campers. She asked me if they could preform the drama in kid's church on a Sunday morning.

"Totally!" I responded. "I'd love that."

She was ecstatic. I didn't ask too many questions. I wanted to let my leaders do what they felt called to do. Kid's church wasn't a place for me to establish my ideas; it was a place for me to encourage and empower everyone's ideas. We had fun doing kid's church this way.

The week had come for Bethann's drama. I had planned on having them preform after worship and announcements. Then, I would follow up the drama with a short message and some prayer time.

I had my flowchart printed out and shared with the leaders who were scheduled. I came into church early to get ready like I always did.

But when I got to the kid's area, I noticed something.

There were no chairs.

Then I noticed there was a set on the stage.

Bethann was running around, moving things back and forth. I was a little disoriented because I hadn't expected to see the room completely taken apart.

I asked Bethann what she was doing.

"We are doing the drama today right?"

"Well, yeah… But we still have to do other things…

How are we going to worship without a stage and where are the kids going to sit?" I asked.

She stopped what she was doing and said,

"I thought we had the whole service…"

Oh no. Miscommunication.

My head spun. Where could she have gotten that idea?

Oh right, ME!

Let's stop for a second.

In this situation, it would've been easy to call this problem a misinterpretation. Misinterpretation is a term used to deflect responsibility and the reality that you played a role in the creating a problem. We need to assume responsibility and our role in the error. This is why I say miscommunication. Don't blame other people for a problem you contributed to creating. Leaders take responsibility even when they don't feel like it's their fault.

Back to the story.

"How long is your drama?" I asked.

"About forty-five minutes."

WHAT!?

I was thinking the drama would be five, maybe ten minutes long.

By my definitions this was not a drama, it was a one-act play!

I don't remember how I exited the conversation, but I somehow excused myself and made it down to my office. How was I going to resolve this situation? I was grasping for answers.

Because I was an independent and capable pastor, once I got to my office, I called my mom.

"Mom! One of my leaders was supposed to do a drama today. I thought it would only be like five or ten minutes and it's almost an hour long!

I have a whole service planned. I already sent the email.

I don't know what to do."

My mom was unfazed by my predicament.

"Casey," she said calmly. "Your volunteer's ideas are just as good as yours."

I gathered my composure and realized that without knowing it, I had slipped into a "submit to me" mindset. I thought my ideas were better.

I thought I was entitled to getting my way because of my position.

I forgot, though I was Bethann's leader, I was also her co-laborer.

I went back to Bethann and apologized for the miscommunication. We got the space ready for the performance. I put aside my agenda and put Bethann's way above my own.

We turned the kids church into a theater.

I have to say, this was one of the best Sundays of the year. The kids loved the drama! The student's involved got to minister with a new medium. Bethann got to work out the kinks before the Royal Family debut. And I got a week to relax and enjoy the ministry as my fellow leaders took the reigns.

I'm not a kid's pastor anymore. I moved into the world of youth ministry. At one youth event, I took part in a leadership seminar led by a man named Johnnie. He brings hundreds of students to an event called National Fine Arts every year. He has, by far, the biggest group there. The logistics of getting nearly five hundred high school students to a week-long talent competition is stressful to even hear about, let alone be in charge of. Yet he does it. He built his entire youth group off of Fine Arts. When asked if he was super passionate about Fine Arts, Johnnie replied, "No, but my students are." I love his perspective so much! He formatted his ministry around what his students were passionate about.

Johnnie says it this way.

"Strategy comes from the stare."

His point was simple. It is not your job as the leader to manipulate everyone in your ministry to get on board with that you're passionate about. It is your job to stare at those you are responsible for and watch for what they are passionate about. When you find their passion, you unify yourself to it.

Because of this revelation in leadership strategy, our youth leaders met together to discuss our next steps as a ministry. We decided that we would spend a month staring. We would spend a month watching and listening for the heartbeat of our students. After the month we reconvened.

In that meeting, one of our youth leaders said, "Our students love worship. If we let them spend hours at the altar, they would."

Everyone agreed.

Another leader said, "I noticed that they love hanging out with each other. They like community. They are a family."

Everyone agreed again.

All of our observations over the month of staring seemed to fall into two trends we called Community and Encounter.

It was time to let the strategy begin!

Worship; alter time, prayer, and convicting messages all fell into ENCOUNTER. These were aspects of our ministry that lent themselves to deeper spiritual connections and experiences. What parts of our service would the students encounter God, in a meaningful and life-changing way?

Games; events, food, and parties all fell into COMMUNITY. We know that no person can grow in their faith outside of community. So, we identified what parts of the ministry were community oriented. What parts of the events would connect the students with one another? What aspects of the service would build friendships and develop community?

The plan was simple; if ENCOUNTER was yellow, and COMMUNITY was blue, what was green?

We focused on developing a green youth ministry. Not just eco-friendly, (though we made that a goal) but one completely focused on what the students were passionate about.

We restructured the entire midweek gathering to begin with a heavy community emphasis; games, food, hang out time, high-energy praise, and comedy.

The ending of the gathering would culminate with deep worship, prayer, convicting messages, and time spent at the altar.

The gatherings developed a seamless transition from one color to the other.

We began focusing on events that were green.

Camp, retreats, worship concerts are all "green" events.

These events all shared a spiritual depth and an opportunity to connect with God and had tons of fun and energy. The youth group exploded. No wonder. It wasn't my youth group. It didn't belong to our volunteer leaders either. The youth group was a manifestation of the very passion God gave to each student individually and the group collectively. Each weekly gathering and every event was a manifestation of the passion of those who attended.

Personally, I would have done it a lot differently. But my way wasn't even an option. We had submitted the direction of the youth group to the youth, and it couldn't have gone any better.

After all, if Jesus, who is God, would submit to his mom's idea, who am I to demand people do as I say? Jesus didn't turn to his mom after her request and say, "Hey, I am in charge. And I am not going to do that right now!"

He didn't think of his agenda as more important than Mary's.

Jesus' agenda to remain hidden and not cause a stir was important.

But Mary's agenda to keep the party going was even more important in that moment.

Read through the Gospels.

Note how, in many cases, Jesus stops mid-agenda to do what someone else wants him to do.

The Woman with the Issue of Blood [6]

The Man at the Pool of Bethesda [7]

Blind Bartimaeus [8]

Zacchaeus [9]

The Centurion's Faith [10]

The Canaanite Woman [11]

There is story after story!

Jesus models how we ought to lead and live. Leadership is not about your ideas or your vision. It's about meeting the needs of those around you. You are anointed in your position to do just as Jesus did.

In Luke 4:18-19, Jesus shares his objective as an anointed leader.

"The Spirit of the Lord is upon me, because he has anointed me to proclaim good news to the poor. He has sent me to proclaim liberty to the captives and recovering of sight to the blind, to set at liberty those who are oppressed, to proclaim the year of the Lord's favor." [12]

Jesus was anointed in a position of authority to proclaim the Gospel, bring freedom, healing, deliverance, and declare the favor of God over people.

The disciples often thought God anointed Jesus to violently establish himself as king; to rule and reign with authority and take what he wanted by force. They couldn't be further from the truth.

Jesus was given a position of authority so he could serve.

Our responsibility as leaders in our churches, communities, schools, and families is the same. When the world pressures you to insist on your own way of doing something and dominate over others, remember Jesus turning water into wine.

Reciprocal submission is vital to our success as leaders. Don't let your desire to have it your way keep you from honoring your brothers and sisters in the faith.

We need to submit to each other as we submit to Christ...

and our moms.

CORNSTALKS

SINGLENESS

PURPOSE

PURSUE YOUR PURPOSE

CHAPTER 10

PURSUE YOUR PURPOSE

Have you ever just needed to shoot a gun?

Maybe it's a guy thing, but occasionally when I'm stressed I just need to destroy something in a controlled environment. It's a good way to vent my anger without punching holes in drywall. Now you think I have an anger problem huh? I don't know exactly why it feels good to trigger a small explosion that propels a piece of lead into a target – but it does.

I called a friend and mentor of mine to see if I could go out to his farm and shoot with him. He happily obliged. So, off to Zell's farm I went.

We talked for a while as we shot at targets fifteen yards away in the soybean field. Half the time we didn't even shoot. We just got carried away in conversation. Turns out, I didn't need to shoot a gun.

I needed to talk to Zell.

Zell has always been present in my life as a person who can calm me down when I get riled up; even when I was a kid at my Junior Bible Quiz meets. I would have panic attacks and Zell would be there to help me come back to reality. So, we talked for a while about all the stuff I was going through as we shot at targets in his field.

He shared his perspective and how he had been praying. I listened. I heard.

Ultimately, I felt better after our gunpowder-scented conversation. As I was walking out in the field to check the targets, I tried to avoid the newly sprouted soybeans. I noticed a corn stalk growing to the left of me. Zell planted corn the year prior. I figured a kernel had survived harvest or perhaps got trapped in the planter. I pointed at the knee-high corn stalk and said, "You've got a corn stalk growing here."

I thought it was cool.

It was certainly unusual to see a cornstalk growing in a bean field.

Zell laughed and said, "That's not a cornstalk."

I looked at him with a puzzled face. I didn't think I was that much of a city boy. I grew up in the Midwest. I think I know what corn looks like.

He looked at the stalk growing up amongst the sprouts.

"That's a weed in a bean field."

When Jesus was walking the earth he was determined to fulfill his purpose. Even as a middle school age kid, Jesus understood his purpose.

"And when he was twelve years old, they went up according to custom. And when the feast was ended, as they were returning, the boy Jesus stayed behind in Jerusalem. His parents did not know it, but supposing him to be in the group they went a day's journey, but then they began to search for him among their relatives and acquaintances, and when they did not find him, they returned to Jerusalem, searching for him. After three days they found him in the temple, sitting among the teachers, listening to them and asking them questions. And all who heard him were amazed at his understanding and his answers. And when his

parents saw him, they were astonished. And his mother said to him, "Son, why have you treated us so? Behold, your father and I have been searching for you in great distress." And he said to them, "Why were you looking for me? Did you not know that I must be in my Father's house?" And they did not understand the saying that he spoke to them. And he went down with them and came to Nazareth and was submissive to them. And his mother treasured up all these things in her heart." [1]

Luke 2:41-51 ESV

I love this story for a few reasons.

1. I think it's funny to imagine Mary and Joseph at the moment they realized they had lost, not only their son, but the Messiah!

2. I like how Jesus and his family took vacations (pilgrimages) with their extended family and friends. I remember my favorite vacations as a child were the ones we took with friends and family.

3. In this story, Jesus made it clear to his parents that he is not like the other kids.

Adolescence is a time of rapid brain development. It is a season of learning through firsthand experience. Teens are notorious for being impulsive and motivated by pleasure.

Every one of us can think back to our teenage years and remember a time where we followed the desire of our flesh into what turned out to be chaotic consequences.

We have all touched the proverbial fire and gotten burned. I don't know about you, but I always knew I was meant to be a pastor. There was just a nagging thought in the back of my head I couldn't avoid.

I tried my best to suppress that thought. I tried my best to reason it away. And yet, here we are.

Eventually, I relented and accepted my purpose.

We can't even imagine a teenager who is so committed to his calling that they don't even let their parents get in the way. That's crazy. Yet, Jesus is twelve and choosing to be in the synagogues. Jesus is about his Father's business. The twelve-year-old Jesus was not motivated by pleasure, but by purpose.

Jesus knew exactly what he was called to do.

Both Mary and Joseph were told what Jesus' destiny was to be as well. You can guarantee that Jesus was not only given a personal understanding of his purpose even as a child, but the prophetic words spoken over his life were also communicated to him by his parents.

In Luke 1 we read about Mary's revelation about her son's destiny.

"In the sixth month of Elizabeth's pregnancy, God sent the angel Gabriel to Nazareth, a town in Galilee, to a virgin pledged to be married to a man named Joseph, a descendant of David. The virgin's name was Mary. The angel went to her and said, "Greetings, you who are highly favored! The Lord is with you." Mary was greatly troubled at his words and wondered what kind of greeting this might be. But the angel said to her, "Do not be afraid, Mary; you have found favor with God. You will conceive and give birth to a son, and you are to call him Jesus. He will be great and will be called the Son of the Most High. The Lord God will give him the throne of his father David, and he will reign over Jacob's descendants forever; his kingdom will never end." [2]

Luke 1:26-33 ESV

Mary knew Jesus' destiny even before he was conceived. His purpose was to establish and reign in God's everlasting kingdom

In Matthew 1 we see how Jesus' purpose was revealed to Joseph.

"Because Joseph her husband was faithful to the law, and yet, did not want to expose her to public disgrace, he had in mind to divorce her quietly. But after he had considered this, an angel of the Lord appeared to him in a dream and said, "Joseph son of David, do not be afraid to take Mary home as your wife, because what is conceived in her is from the Holy Spirit. She will give birth to a son, and you are to give him the name Jesus, because he will save his people from their sins." All this took place to fulfill what the Lord had said through the prophet: "The virgin will conceive and give birth to a son, and they will call him Immanuel" (which means "God with us")." [3]

Matthew 1:19-23 ESV

Joseph understood that Jesus was destined to save all of us from our sin. Jesus was the Savior of the world!

Both Jesus and his parents knew what he was called to do. Jesus never deviated from that path, though time and time again he was offered an easier road. Jesus pursued his purpose and pushed through.

Immediately following a revelation of personal purpose, we get amped up!

Have you ever realized your destiny and become passionate about it?

You think about it all the time. You are eager. You are excited.

But, as any student who has ever gone to a summer camp can tell you, the mountaintop experience doesn't go on forever.

We often feel God's presence so tangibly, and zealously dedicate ourselves to him, but when the monotony of everyday life begins to swaddle and rock us, we drift back to sleep and settle for our dreams instead of our destiny. It's hard to stay motivated. It's challenging to stay on task. Though difficult, it is necessary in the pursuit of purpose that we hold fast to what God has called us toward. We must stay on the path to our purpose.

The simple truth is, very few things are in inherently good or bad.

Everything helps serve a purpose.

Is marriage good? Depends.

Is it okay to get a tattoo? Maybe, maybe not.

Is it a sin to drink alcohol? Potentially.

Are Chick-Fil-A nuggets good? Yes. That one gets a solid yes.

The point of holiness is to be living in obedience to God. God clearly commands his people in Leviticus 19:2 saying, **"You shall be holy, for I the Lord your God am holy."** [4]

What does that mean?

It means you shall live in a way that is distinct from other people.

You are called to a life that is individually reflective of Jesus. It's not a list of do's and don'ts. It's a simple command to be like Jesus.

God is saying, "Be different, like me."

Paul talks about how we ought to live with a determined focus on our purpose.

In 1 Corinthians 7 he gives us the person al example of marriage. Paul knew what he was called to do, and like Jesus, he would not let anything, even a good thing, get in the way. He says in 1 Corinthians 7:7-9,

YOU DO NOT NEED TO HAVE A RING ON YOUR FINGER TO HAVE A CALLING IN YOUR HEART.

"I wish that all were as I myself am. But each has his own gift from God, one of one kind and one of another. To the unmarried and the widows I say that it is good for them to remain single, as I am. But if they cannot exercise self-control, they should marry. For it is better to marry than to burn with passion." [5]

He continues in verse 17,

"Only let each person lead the life that the Lord has assigned to him, and to which God has called him. This is my rule in all the churches." [6]

In verse 32-35, he explains why.

"I want you to be free from anxieties. The unmarried man is anxious about the things of the Lord, how to please the Lord. But the married man is anxious about worldly things, how to please his wife, and his interests are divided. And the unmarried or betrothed woman is anxious about the things of the Lord, how to be holy in body and spirit. But the married woman is anxious about worldly things, how to please her husband. I say this for your own benefit, not to lay any restraint upon you, but to promote good order and to secure your undivided devotion to the Lord." [7]

Is marriage bad?

After reading what Paul was instructing the church to do, we may say that we shouldn't encourage marriage. But that's not the point Paul is making.

He is saying that a life fully devoted to Christ is the goal.

Each of us has a different calling. If marriage makes it more difficult to follow that calling, we should remain single. If being single makes it more difficult to follow our calling, we should get married.

One is not greater than the other.

The focus is obedience to what God has created us to do.

I am a single guy.

I can honestly say I am thankful for my singleness. The opportunities I have to minister and build community are greatly increased by my relationship status.

Am I called to be single forever? I don't think so. It doesn't matter. My goal isn't to get married. My goal is to be like Jesus.

In this season of ministry, a relationship would be a hindrance for me. While taking a group of the boys I mentor out to eat, they asked me why I was single. I told them, "Do you think I would be hanging out with you guys and buying you food all the time if I was dating someone?" One answered, "True... you should stay single."

He was only thinking about free Chick-Fil-A. I don't blame him at all.

Free Chick-Fil-A is the best Chick-Fil-A.

I love building relationships with my dozens of "little brothers". I love getting to mentor them the same way that my mentors mentored me – through relationship. I think back to those youth leaders who spent time with me and invested into me relationally and I can't express my gratitude. I want to be that figure to the students God has allowed me to influence.

I know what my purpose is, and in this season, it is a good thing that I am single.

Honestly, I've read a lot of books on ministry and church leadership and this subject is clearly avoided. Why? Singleness is valueable! In our American culture, where an ideal life includes a loving spouse and 2.5 kids, singleness has become some sort of disease. I feel like a leper in certain circles. I feel like people pity me. I feel like I don't have legitimacy until I have a wife.

What a ridiculous notion!

How crazy is it that I've been a pastor for almost a decade and I still don't feel like an adult around other pastors (some younger than me) who are married?

As I talk with my single friends, the feeling isn't exclusive to me.

I know many single people involved in ministry who feel like they have been discredited or dishonored because of their relationship status. They feel like they aren't treated with respect or appreciation simply because they aren't married.

So, to all my single friends reading this.

I want you to know something.

You lack NOTHING.

You do not need to have a ring on your finger to have a calling in your heart.

I'm sorry people treat you so weird.

You are uniquely placed in your current position to be like Jesus. There is a teenager in your life who need you to show them what it looks like to pursue Jesus without being married. How else would they know it's possible, if every spiritual influence in their life is married? They need you to model a Christ-focused singleness to them. Encourage them. Show them how they don't need a relationship to have joy, purpose, and value!

Show the young women they don't need a boy to know they are beautiful and special!

Show the young men they don't need a girl to be strong and confident.

Show them what it looks like to find your worth and identity in none but Jesus!

Have you ever stopped to think about why Jesus never married?

I think the simple answer is that he didn't have time. He was too busy. He had a purpose to die for the sins of the world and totally redeem all of humanity. And he was not going to let a romantic relationship with a woman steal his focus. I believe Jesus was modeling the simple truth that even good things can become a hindrance to what God has called you to do.

Even eating a Chick-Fil-A sandwich becomes a problem while you're fasting.

Thank God for the Mother Theresa's and Henri Nouwen's of the world! Thank God for the people who have embraced the single life and lived it well.

The purpose of any one person is not to become one with another, but to become one with Christ.

Marriage is a beautiful thing. It is a covenant that symbolizes the self-sacrifice of Christ for his bride, and us for him. It is reciprocated love and affection between two people. It is the institution through which we raise families and train the next generation of world changers. Marriage is the foundation of the family. It is necessary to the expansion of the church.

But above that.

Above marriage.

Above family.

Above symbolism.

Above all, is Christ and to be like him.

This is the purpose of the created, to be like the Creator.

My prayer for those of you reading is that you become like Christ.

That is your original purpose.

Don't get sidetracked.

Run fast and hard toward the goal of becoming like Jesus.

If you notice a cute girl or handsome guy running next to you, run together. Believe me, I feel like I look over my shoulder quite a bit to see who's running next to me. Maybe I'll see someone around the next turn. It doesn't change my speed. It doesn't change my direction. Jesus is my focus. I am content to have no one else for the rest of my life. If that sounds strange to you, perhaps you've let your fantasies about a romantic relationship overshadow the real reason you are alive; to be like Jesus!

Paul says in Philippians 3:14, **"I press on toward the goal to win the prize for which God has called me heavenward in Christ Jesus.** [8]

You will be given many opportunities to pursue "good" things on your journey toward your purpose.

But, when those "good" things steer you off course, they become hindrances.

This can happen in many different areas in our lives – not only relationships.

Our finances.

Our jobs.

Our homes.

Our friends.

Our hobbies.

They can all steer us away from our purpose when left unchecked. Good things can keep us from Jesus when they become our pursuit.

Jesus modeled a resolute focus on the goal ahead of him. He knew what he needed to accomplish, and he pursued it with tenacity and determination.

As the prophet Isaiah would say he, **"set his face like flint"**. [9]

Jesus valued the determined pursuit of purpose. I am not going to look away from the calling that God has for me.

Nothing will change my course.

When we allow good things to steer us in the wrong direction, they become problems.

It's no longer a healthy relationship; it's a hindrance that changes your purpose.

It's no longer a promotion at work; it's a taskmaster that keeps you from whole-heartedly serving God.

It's no longer your hometown; it's a comfort zone keeping you stagnate.

It's no longer your social media platform; it's an idol stealing your attention.

It's no longer a financial blessing, it's an addiction to the next best thing.

It's no longer a corn stalk; it's a weed in a bean field.

PURSUE YOUR PURPOSE

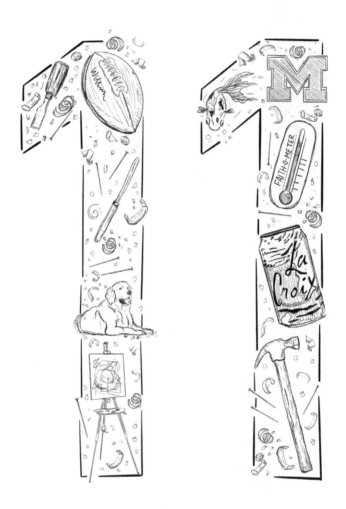

LA CROIX

JOBS

DOING GOOD

DO GOOD, WHENEVER, WHEREVER

CHAPTER 11

DO GOOD, WHATEVER, WHEREVER

I've been a children's pastor, youth pastor, worship leader, author, intern, evangelist, missionary, teacher, coach, artist, consultant, server, caterer, graphic designer, etc....

And I've only been in ministry for a decade!

Ministry is a wide word. When I talk to people about what they do, they find the most descriptive and exclusive term to define it.

"I'm a youth pastor."

"I'm a teacher."

"I'm a salesman."

What we do often describes who we are. If you are an administrative assistant or a math teacher, I will assume you are someone who prefers order and systems.

If you are an artist or a barista, I assume you like to have fun and aren't as detailed oriented as your administrative brothers and sisters.

Of course, there are people who bend these norms. But norms are fairly reliable predictors. That's why they are called norms. A norm is what tends to be more often than not. The trouble comes when we identify with the traits of what we do, rather than the purpose of why we do it.

I coach football.

I like football, but I'm not a super fan.

I watch the Super Bowl and the Michigan, Ohio State game. (Which is a huge deal where I'm from) Beyond that, I don't really care about the world of football.

I coach football because as our head coach, Bill says,

"Football is the ultimate team sport."

I really love helping young men become strong, brave, men of God who devote themselves to one another. Football requires every person on the team to give their best effort. Everyone depends on everyone. Every touchdown depends on the entire team as a unit. The receiver only catches a ball if the quarterback throws it well. The quarterback can only throw a good pass if he has good pass protection from the line. The line can only give the quarterback time if the backs are running the linebackers out of the box.

Football is about the team.

I coach football to disciple students. The game comes second. I love winning. I love celebrating excellence on and off the field. I especially love making my linemen do up downs and drill on the five-man sled.

(Shout out to my O-line!)

I like to help students push themselves to become better. When I coach football, I feel a sense of purpose. I'm doing some good. My purpose is to be like Jesus. Football is a means by which I fulfill that purpose.

I am also an artist.

I don't sell my art.

I don't have an exhibit.

I just like to create.

It's okay to identify with the work you do outside of your vocation. Creating is fundamental in human nature. God is a creator. We are made in his image. It stands to reason that we would have a bit of the creative gene. Art has always been such an enjoyable method of expressing my inner creativity. There is nothing quite like making something out of nothing. Even if you're not very good at it.

We all need to remember Mr. Rogers' perspective on creating things.

"Do you like to draw with crayons? I do. But I'm not very good at it. But it doesn't matter. It's just the fun of doing it that's important..." [1]

Fred Rogers

The purpose of art is to participate in the character of our Creator. We create good, in a world where what we have created did not previously exist.

I have thousands of La Croix cans in my garage. You may think I have a problem. I think I have a masterpiece in the works.
Both may be true.

I am saving them, not to recycle though...

(In Michigan, you get 10 cents for every recycled can.)

I am saving them to make something. I don't know what I want to do yet, but I have a few ideas. I have a koi pond in my backyard. I don't use it yet...

Yet...

My favorite idea is to disassemble the cans and make them flat sheets of aluminum. Then, I will cover the koi pond with the La Croix sheets. Thus transforming this average koi pond into a one of a kind La Croix pond!

I know, it's brilliant!

It's a little out of the box. It may not be practical, but it is creative! And that's the whole point! It's about being creative. I want to create. If the idea of a La Croix pond makes someone laugh or even smirk at how clever or silly the idea is – it is well worth the time spent dreaming it up. I have done my job if I make even just one person smile while we talk about my dream of a La Croix pond. I've brought a little bit of good into the world. I haven't even done it yet. It's still just a thought.

But even a creative thought can inspire and bring joy.

This is why I like telling stories. There is something special about creating worlds and characters. I love leading people through the worlds I create in my stories. I am fascinated by the collective imagination story telling produces. I think that's why I love the Bible so much. The Bible is the story of God. He created his own world and characters. He fills it with stories and invites us to imagine new stories with him.

Jesus is the ultimate story teller.

Romans 11:36 says, **"For from him and through him and to him are all things. To him be glory forever. Amen."** [2]

We need to remember that Jesus was a part of the creation story.

He was there at the beginning, bringing life out of dust with the Father and Holy Spirit.

"In the beginning, God created the heavens and the earth. The earth was without form and void, and darkness was over the face of the deep. And the Spirit of God was hovering over the face of the waters. And God said, "Let there be light," and there was light." [3]

Genesis 1:1-3 ESV

The first verse highlights the Father. Creator God. Elohim. The God above all gods.

The second verse emphasizes the Holy Spirit. The Helper. The One holding it all together.

The third verse focuses on the Word. The very Logos of the Godhead. Jesus. The Yes and Amen of Creation.

The Apostle John was given revelation as to who this Word was. He writes his understanding in of John 1.

"In the beginning was the Word, and the Word was with God, and the Word was God. He was with God in the beginning. Through him all things were made; without him nothing was made that has been made. In him was life, and that life was the light of all mankind. The light shines in the darkness, and the darkness has not overcome it." [4]

John 1:1-5 ESV

Jesus is the Word spoken at creation. He is involved in every bit of the process.

In the beginning, Jesus brought goodness out of nothingness. God looked at the blank canvas and created something good.

It is no wonder that when Jesus became flesh and lived as a human, he worked as a craftsman. He continued to create.

He worked with his hands to create things that were both beautiful and practical.

The same God that created the mountains, and the sea was sanding and carving patterns into wooden tables and chairs.

He made good out of nothing.

He brought light from dark.

He built a table from a fallen tree.

The purpose of creation is simple; to create something good.

WHEN WE BOX OURSELVES INTO THE DESCRIPTION OF WHAT WE DO, WE RISK NEGLECTING WHAT SOMEONE REALLY NEEDS.

It's what Jesus does every day.

It's what we should do every day.

We like to identify with certain types of creation. We create youth ministries. We create lesson plans.

We create _____ (fill in the blank).

But what happens when someone doesn't need what you create?

When we box ourselves into the description of what we do, we risk neglecting what someone really needs.

As a football coach, I motivate the players to push themselves. I tell them to leave it all on the field. They need to give a hundred and ten percent. There will be time to rest after practice.

But, when a student of mine is struggling with something personal, they don't need to run sprints. They need me to listen. They need to know God is with them. They need to know someone cares.

Matthew 15 tells one of the most peculiar stories of the New Testament.

"And Jesus went away from there and withdrew to the district of Tyre and Sidon. And behold, a Canaanite woman from that region came out and was crying, "Have mercy on me, O Lord, Son of David; my daughter is severely oppressed by a demon." But he did not answer her a word. And his disciples came and begged him, saying, "Send her away, for she is crying out after us." He answered, "I was sent only to the lost sheep of the house of Israel." But she came and knelt before him, saying, "Lord, help me." And he answered, "It is not right to take the children's bread and throw it to the dogs." She said, "Yes, Lord, yet even the dogs eat the crumbs that fall from their masters' table." Then Jesus answered her, "O woman, great is your faith! Be it done for you as you desire." And her daughter was healed instantly." [5]

Matthew 15:21-28 ESV

In this story, a woman comes with a serious request for Jesus. Her daughter is demon oppressed. The woman knows that Jesus can deliver her daughter. There are a few problems facing this woman, however.

1. She is a woman.

In this place and time, it was not right for a woman to approach a man.

2. She was a Canaanite.

This woman comes from the former inhabitants of the land of Israel. She is not a part of God's chosen people. There is a strong racial prejudice present.

3. She has interrupted something.

We don't know the exact scene, but we can infer from the disciple's response that she is intruding. She is annoying them.

Jesus is aware of all the roadblocks in her way. From the second he sees her; he is impressed by her faith. He knows what she is risking to talk to him. He knows that this is not comfortable for her. Jesus also knows that she has counted the costs and has come ready to get what she wants. She won't leave empty-handed. So, Jesus addresses these issues.

He says, "That's not my job. I wasn't sent here to deliver Canaanites."

She asked again.

He responds once more, "Why would I give to you what belongs to the children of God? You're not a Jew. You know you have no claim in the inheritance of Heaven."

The woman responded meekly, "True, however, I'm not asking for an inheritance, I just need a touch and I'll be on my way."

Upon hearing the woman rattle back, you can almost see Jesus beam with pride. "I've never seen someone with such great faith. You will get what you need."

I used to think Jesus was being rude. That's not the case at all.

I think he knew the woman was not going to give up. Sometimes you can see the resilience in people. I believe Jesus was playing this out to teach us, not her. He knew she didn't need a lesson. She needed a miracle. The disciples needed a lesson. Jesus responded to the woman with the disciple's mentality. He was participating in prophetic theater so he could teach a lesson.

The lesson being taught was simple. Even though we have our so-called "callings", the actual reason we are here is to do just as Jesus did in the beginning of creation and in this story.

We create light in the darkness.

We do good.

Jesus addressed all the reasons the disciples were thinking would justify turning this woman away. They listened to Jesus bring up each reason why not and nodded their heads in agreement.

Then the woman responded with faith.

The disciples were not ready for Jesus to respond the way he did.

They expected Jesus to rebuke the woman and get back to whatever they were doing. Jesus taught the disciples, right then and there about their purpose.

They are to do good; forgetting all the reasons why not to do good, and just do good.

We can always think of a hundred reasons why not to do something good for someone. But only one reason is needed to do it.

Jesus would do it.

Could you imagine if one of my football players asked me for help on their homework and I responded, "That's not my job"? Or what if my brother asked me for help painting his house and I said, "I'm not a painter". It doesn't matter what your "job" is, it matters that you do good. Step out of your job description.

People were so often confused by Jesus because he consistently did things that people didn't think the Messiah would do. He spent time with the poor and the hurting. He befriended sinners and outcasts. He took naps in boats. He retreated into the wilderness for lengthy periods of time. He touched lepers! He didn't show interest in gaining political power. He didn't like violence. He loved little kids. He didn't conform to his so-called job description. He did good wherever he was.

We are agents of good in this hurting world. Jesus wanted the disciples, and us to know that our job descriptions are just that; descriptions of our jobs, not descriptions of purpose.

There is no reason big enough to keep us from doing good for someone.

Being like Jesus means doing good; whatever that is, wherever we are.

GAS TANKS
PRAYER
SURVIVOR (AGAIN)

STAY FILLED UP IN PRAYER

CHAPTER 12

STAY FILLED UP IN PRAYER

Living like Jesus doesn't only require us to focus on others; it requires us to take care of ourselves.

It is very easy to twist the idea of loving yourself and caring for yourself and make it about feeding your flesh. It's not about feeding your flesh at all.

True self-care isn't hedonism; true self-care is wisdom.

After all, an empty cup can't pour much out. If we truly want to be like Jesus, we must take time to make sure we are well. Caring for yourself is not about satisfying your every desire. It's not the motto Treat Yo Self like from the T.V. show Parks and Recreation. Caring for oneself is a discipline of a healthy believer.

The world says self-care means giving into your every fleshly desire, being impulsive, and splurging on temporal things. That is the opposite of the truth!

True self-care is more like developing a healthy diet and exercise plan. Developing a healthy lifestyle requires discipline, strength, and a firm commitment.

Becoming unhealthy emotionally, spiritually, and physically is a major hindrance to the spread of the Gospel. It is easy to get caught up in going through the motions, serving, and working for the cause of the kingdom, while ignoring your personal health.

I've been guilty of this myself. I took on far too much work, and it caused me to spiral into panic attacks, exhaustion, and even apathy about ministry. I was working too much and resting too little.

It is hard to isolate yourself and rest when you are an extrovert. But, I've also found that it is hard to work out in the gym consistently. But I still do it. Because I want to be healthy.

I love being busy. It's hard to slow down. I need to intentionally find time to be alone. It is in the isolation that the Spirit revitalizes your soul.

It doesn't matter what your personality type is, you need to spend some time alone with Jesus.

The COVID-19 pandemic was a difficult time for me initially. I was worried that I wouldn't be able to manage not being out and about, hanging out with friends, going to church, or eating at foodie restaurants. Yet, as I woke up every day of the social distancing period, I was greeted by the sweet fragrance of an empty schedule. I would wake up at 8:00 am and get around for the day. I would pour myself a cup of coffee and spend time with the Lord. It was like a reset. I realized, I don't need hurry. I need to spend time with Jesus.

I was taking our youth group to Cedar Point. We had about thirty students going in three different vehicles. I was driving the shuttle bus. If you don't know what Cedar Point is, I want you to imagine your favorite amusement park, and then just picture it bigger and better.

Maybe I'm biased.

But, I truly believe that Cedar Point's roller coasters are better than anywhere else in the world. As far as I'm concerned, Cedar Point is the best amusement park on the face of the earth.

Anyway, we spent a full day up there riding rides and waiting in lines.

Honestly, we spent a lot more time waiting in lines than we did riding rides. That's how it goes, I suppose. I enjoyed myself, but I still had a mission.

My mission was twofold:

1. Don't lose any students

and

2. Get home on time.

IT DOESN'T MATTER WHAT YOUR PERSONALITY TYPE IS, YOU NEED TO SPEND SOME TIME ALONE WITH JESUS.

A modest pair of goals, I know. But, in an amusement park that literally inhabits its own peninsula with thousands of people running around, I feel like it's a win if I can at least get them all home and at a reasonable time.

I had my itinerary.

I had my system.

I had my communicated plan.

I was ready to have fun on the trip, but when the time came, I was ready to get home on time with all the same kids I left with. No more, no less.

Especially no less.

It was time to leave the park. The students and leaders all met up at the meeting spot.

All except a few students…

I was getting a little antsy as I asked all the other students and leaders where the missing group was. Apparently, they were caught on a broken down ride…

Or so I was told.

We waited and waited. It felt like an hour had passed. It had really only been a few minutes. (A few minutes feels like an hour to a person with a strict itinerary.)

"Ok, everyone is here now. Let's count and go."

I budgeted time for something like this. As I counted again, I realized we were still missing some students. While we were waiting for the late group, another group got bored and walked into the Starbucks next to the meeting spot. Now we had to wait for them to get their drinks. The extra time I had built into the schedule was quickly disappearing. Oh, youth ministry... If we were going to make the arrival time, we needed to leave as soon as possible!

Eventually we were all aboard the vans. Off we went.

I felt like the Holy Spirit was telling me to take the back way home.

I obeyed. Thank God! I figured The Lord was directing me a different way to avoid traffic on the freeway. About thirty minutes into the trip, the steering started locking up and the shuttle started slowing down. I looked at my gages. I checked for blinking lights. Then I saw the orange needle drooping toward the letter E.

I had run out of gas.

We were stranded on an old back road in rural Ohio.

Better stranded on the back road than the highway, though.

It was about a ten-minute drive to the nearest gas station. I had the other drivers continue on to the church so they would be home on time. I figured it's better to have just a few students late than all of them.

I didn't have roadside assistance, and the tall cornfield next to us was giving off Children of the Corn vibes, so I called the police for help. They could bring us gas and protect us against whatever was in the creepy corn field.

After about an hour, a policeman showed up. I got out of the driver's seat, walked up to the cruiser, and thanked him for coming. He asked if I had a gas can.

"Uh no… I thought you would bring one."

I didn't want to sound ungrateful, but what was he doing responding to a call about a bus stranded on the side of the road without a gallon of gas in hand.

Why even come? What help did he have to give with no gas?

He decided to stay with us on the roadside and call for another cop to come help us with the gas. Though I thought the idea was less than stellar, and it would've been much easier if he just went to get gas with my credit card, I agreed indifferently.

We waited another hour for the next squad car to bring us gas.

The next cop showed up, and I got out to greet her. I thanked her for coming to help. I asked for the gas.

She didn't bring gas either!

So, just to recap, we have been stranded on the side of the road for two hours waiting for the help of two cops, neither of whom brought any gas!

I don't know why they even came!

The second officer said she could take one of the students with her to the gas station about ten miles up the road to get a gas can and fill it up. I thought, "Why didn't the first guy just do that?"

With my teeth tightly clinched down on my tongue, I sent a student with her.

I chose Cole to go.

I was confident that he would be the least likely of the boys in the bus to spend the cash on candy and energy drinks.

We waited for Cole, and his new police chauffeur to return with the gas. It's sad, but to be honest, I wasn't a hundred percent convinced that this duo could nail the task.

The cruiser pulled up with a little red can full of gas.

I jokingly jeered, "What's this? We needed diesel."

That would've been mean.

I thanked the two police officers and emptied the container into the tank. The little red can provided us with just enough gas to make it to the station down the road.

We made it home only three hours past the original ETA.

Living like Jesus means that you spend time every day filling up. You keep your soul heath a key focus in your daily life. We can't afford to get stranded on the side of the road after every Sunday service. We can't run out of gas after every day at work. It is easy to preach about. It is less easy to practice.

Running out of gas isn't very good for your engine.

We can't depend on an emergency fill up because we neglected to spend the necessary time in isolation and prayer. Here's a simple rhyme to remember.

Get away and pray every day.

My inner kid's pastor just came out right there.

Jesus was one of the busiest people ever to walk the earth. He had the most jam-packed ministry and did more than any other person on the planet.

And his ministry only lasted three years!

Jesus had a secret.

It wasn't actually a secret.

It is public information.

Luke makes mention to this frequent practice in Luke 5:16,

"But he would withdraw to desolate places and pray." [1]

Some translations emphasize the repetitive nature of Jesus' intentional isolation.

Mark catches Jesus in the act early one morning on another occasion.

"And rising very early in the morning, while it was still dark, he departed and went out to a desolate place, and there he prayed." [2]

Mark 1:35 ESV

Matthew also notices Jesus isolating himself to pray.

"And after he had dismissed the crowds, he went up on the mountain by himself to pray. When evening came, he was there alone" [3]

Matthew 14:23 ESV

If Jesus needed to get alone and pray, we do to.

Too often we try to do too much while neglecting to allow God to fill up our tank in prayer. We need to spend time alone praying if we want to stay healthy.

Prayer is not stop and go. It is stop and stay.

Everything else can wait.

Connecting to the Father through isolated prayer has got to be the most important thing on your schedule. If it isn't, change your schedule.

It is that simple.

Too many people live and give out of lack. If you have too many responsibilities and not enough time, either make time or free yourself of some responsibilities.

Martin Luther is credited with saying, "I have so much to do that I shall spend the first three hours in prayer."

He understood the importance of prayer.

I mentioned in Chapter 1 how much I love the show Survivor.

If anyone reading this works in casting, please call me!

Jeff often begins the show with the contestants on a boat offshore. He tells the future castaways that they have one minute to salvage what they can from a boat before they get on their rafts and row to the island.

I love watching this frantic scene on T.V. Each person is sprinting around the boat to find something of value.

Some people grab nets or knives.

Others grab chickens or coconuts.

I think I would grab fishing supplies. It would be something that would help me in the long run.

Although I will admit, if I noticed a chest full of coffee beans, I would let go of everything else and grab as much coffee as I could.

Here's the thing.

We often treat prayer like that first episode of Survivor. We wake up in the morning and say a quick prayer. Maybe we read a devotional or a bible verse. Doing this is like grabbing just one thing from the boat. But in God's show, there is the option to dock the boat at shore and have access to everything on the boat for the duration of your stay.

We don't need to frantically approach God with what little time we have left in a busy day and ask him for one morsel of sustenance. We can instead spend time alone with God and receive literally everything we need from him.

Jesus tells us

"And whatever you ask in prayer, you will receive, if you have faith." [4]

Matthew 21:22 ESV

Jesus isn't pulling our leg.

He is telling us the key to his fruitful ministry.

Jesus had everything he needed for his ministry because of the time he spent receiving those things in prayer.

If we want to be like Jesus, we need to spend time, (a significant amount of time) in prayer.

SOCCER

FENCES

PREJUDICE

PUT UP WELCOME SIGNS, NOT FENCES

CHAPTER 13

PUT UP WELCOME SIGNS, NOT FENCES

My family is NOT a soccer family.

We play baseball.

My dad played major league ball, and has made his career coaching baseball. Two of his brothers played minor league ball and coach as well. My grandpa John is a Hall of Fame coach after years of coaching college ball. He also coached with Team Italy in multiple Olympics!

With a genes like that, soccer was never really a thought. My dad always encouraged us to play his favorite sports outside of base-ball season: football, basketball, and tennis. We were dissuaded from playing soccer. My dad has respect for soccer. I just don't think he wanted to sit through a game where scoring is so rare. I know for a fact that he hated the infamous soccer flops.

Who wants to watch a bunch of people chase a ball around for an hour?

Not my family.

Because I never played soccer as a kid, I grew up thinking the sport was pretty lame.

Over the past few years, however, I have learned how to enjoy and appreciate a soccer game. The college I attended didn't have foot-ball, just soccer.

So, I had no choice but to learn to like soccer.

I found that I was pretty prejudice against the sport.

I thought my favorite sports were better. I thought anyone who played soccer was a sissy. I held firm to this belief for a while.

It's a relatively harmless thing to be prejudice against. It doesn't matter much in the grand scheme of things.

I was group leading at FaHoLo Camp (an Assemblies of God District Camp). It was probably around my fifth year working at the camp. I had a pretty good idea on what I was doing. By this time in my camp group-leading career, I was one of the veterans. I didn't worry about much. I was comfortable in my position. I knew how to handle most every situation I might encounter.

Remember, pride comes before the fall.

I was talking about sports with some boys in my group. Most fourth and fifth grade boys like sports. They often have a favorite sport and a favorite team, of which they tend to be fanatical. As we were talking about sports, one boy, Gabe, spoke up and said that he played soccer.

I said something like, "Oh soccer! Are you not old enough to play a real sport?"

I don't know exactly what I said, but it was teetering on the line between a light-hearted quip and rude remark.

Gabe took it the best way he could and joked back about how boring baseball was to watch.

He had a point.

Perhaps I hadn't considered how boring it must be to watch baseball with noidea of what was going on. I joked back a little more, and we sparred for a minute or two around the subject. After our reciprocal roasting session, things went back to normal.

"I guess I just don't like soccer." I said as we ended the conversation.

We went about the rest of the day with no problems and no concerns.

I was focused back on the task at hand – camp.

The service that night was so powerful. Kids all over the camp were being touched by God in the exact way they needed. The specific focus was on the calling of God on each of the kid's lives. God calls us all to different things. Not one calling is better than another. We are all a part of the Body of Christ. Each of us serves a different function. We need each other to operate in unique ways.

A body made up of just arms can't do much for the kingdom.

In fact, it will probably just scare people away.

It's a terrifying thought if you really think about it.

The next day we were in line for breakfast and I was going around my group asking the kids about what they learned at the service the night before.

I asked them the question, "What did God call you to do with your life?"

This question is a huge question, especially for kids. But it's good for them to start thinking about the answer even when they are young. They don't have time to waste. If they have a goal, it's never too early to start going after it.

One kid would say, "I think God wants me to be a pastor."

Another would say, "God told me to become a teacher."

The kids went around and shared their callings with one another. I looked at Gabe, who was normally very interested in sharing his experiences with the group. But for some reason, was quiet this morning.

"What about you, Gabe? What did God call you to be?" I smiled as I waited for his response.

I'm sure he would be called to ministry in one form or another. He was a special kid with tons of energy and confidence, clearly destined to do great things.

He still is.

I knew God would use him in a big way. Gabe just lowered his head. I could see he was uncomfortable talking about his calling.

Then he quietly said, "God called me to be a soccer player."

My heart sank.

He stood there looking at me like he had offended me. I immediately regretted my silly debate. I thought we were just kidding around.

I didn't know that I was bashing the very thing Gabe loves more than anything else.

I was crushed. I had felt like I just invalidated a kid's dream.

More than that, I invalidated a call of God!

In John 4 there is a story about Jesus' encounter with a woman at a well.

Jesus was passing through Samaria when he stopped upon a well. This well once belonged to the Israelites. Now it was the watering hole of the Samaritans.

> **JESUS DIDN'T PUT UP THESE FENCES LIKE WE DO; HE TORE THEM DOWN AND PUT UP FLASHING NEON WELCOME SIGNS.**

The Samaritans were essentially half Jew, half Gentile. There was a strong prejudice the Jewish people had toward them. It was out of the norm for a Jew to pass through Samaria at all, let alone stop and drink the water.

Jesus goes even further than just stopping at the well. As he approached the well, he saw a Samaritan woman. He didn't ignore her. He engaged her in conversation.

"Could you pour me some water? I'm parched." Jesus said with a smile.

She was aware of the circumstances and responded to his invitation to conversation by saying, "Why are you talking to me? I am a Samaritan woman."

Jesus wasn't concerned that she didn't understand him. He said, "There are a lot of things you don't understand, I'm one of those things. See, if you knew who I was, you would ask me for the living water that I offer. Water that if you just drink once, you will never thirst again."

"Ok," The woman said slowly. "I'll take some of the water you have. I hate having to come here every day and draw water from this old well."

Jesus said, "Ok, go home and grab your husband and I'll give you both the water I have."

The woman's head hung low. She said, "I don't have a husband."

Jesus smiled and said, "I know. You have had five husbands, and the man you're living with right now isn't your husband."

The woman was shocked.

"You're a prophet, aren't you?" she said as a matter of fact.

She inquired, "You're a Jew. I'm a Samaritan. Our ancestors used to worship God here on this mountain. You say it's better to worship God in the city."

Jesus responded, "There is coming a day when people will worship God in spirit, rather than in a certain location."

"You're talking about the Messiah." she said with understanding in her voice.

Jesus replied, "I am the Messiah."

The woman was shaken to her core.

She believed.

The Messiah had visited her and even though he knew everything she had ever done, he still wanted to have a relationship with her. He offered her access to the Father. She ran home to her town and told everyone what had happened. Curious, they ran out to the well to meet with Jesus.

I'll let you read the rest of the story as written.

"Many Samaritans from that town believed in him because of the woman's testimony, "He told me all that I ever did." So when the Samaritans came to him, they asked him to stay with them, and he stayed there two days. And many more believed because of his word. They said to the woman, "It is no longer because of what you said that we believe, for we have heard for ourselves, and we know that this is indeed the Savior of the world." After the two days he departed for Galilee. (For Jesus himself had testified that a prophet has no honor in his own hometown.) So when he came to Galilee, the Galileans welcomed him, having seen all that he had done in Jerusalem at the feast. For they too had gone to the feast." [1]

John 4:39-45 ESV

Jesus stayed with the Samaritans for two days. He broke down a very prevalent racial barrier in that time and place.

I read this story often from the perspective of a disciple.

What was going on in Peter's head during all of this?

He must have been thinking, "Why is Jesus talking to a Samaritan woman?"

One of them muttered under their breath, "Come on Jesus… let's get out of this place. I hate Samaria. I feel dirty just standing here."

Their prejudices were as heightened and apparent as they would have ever been. And just when they thought they were about to leave and go back home, Jesus decides to spend the night!

I can't even imagine how uncomfortable that must have been for the disciples.

Jesus doesn't have prejudices; just a whole lot of love.

Because Jesus was able to overlook the stigma and the taboo cultural biases, this woman and her whole town could believe. They received the Gospel because Jesus was willing to break down the wall of prejudice and enter into a relationship with people who were not like him.

We often think of prejudice in terms of race. Race is clearly an issue being addressed in this story! The Jewish disciples felt that they had a superior race to the Samaritans. They felt like they were better simply because they were born to a certain set of parents. Jesus rejects their racial prejudices. Jesus loves regardless of race or background. But if we believe that prejudice is only present in the realm of race, we are mistaken.

We can have prejudice in all areas of our life. It happens when we think the variables that make us unique are intrinsically better than the things that make others unique. Prejudice rejects the beauty of diversity.

We need to address this sin in all areas of our lives. We need to open ourselves up to new experiences. We must engage people who are different than we are and learn to appreciate the things that make them, well, not us. We befriend people different from us and learn to like what they like. This is why I have a rule to never order chicken strips at a restaurant.

In 1 Corinthians 9, Paul writes,

"For though I am free from all, I have made myself a servant to all, that I might win more of them. To the Jews I became as a Jew, in order to win Jews. To those under the law I became as one under the law (though not being myself under the law) that I might win those under the law. To those outside the law I became as one outside the law (not being outside the law of God but under the law of Christ) that I might win those outside the law. To the weak I became weak, that I might win the weak. I have become all things to all people, that by all means I might save some. I do it all for the sake of the gospel, that I may share with them in its blessings." [2]

1 Corinthians 9:19-23 ESV

Paul understood that in order to be like Jesus you have to put aside your preferences.

I used to think I was being authentic when I shared about things I liked and disliked. I thought it was inauthentic to try to like everything.

It is not inauthentic; it's called trying to relate to people.

Jesus put aside his preferences and engaged with people on their ground. He didn't try to find common ground; he just stepped onto their ground.

How many people are not hearing the Gospel because we simply built walls around ourselves?

How many people will never hear the Gospel because we made up our mind where we will not go?

How many people will die without knowing Jesus because we continue to hold on to our prejudices?

We put fences around our lives like we put fences around our houses, and for the same reason. We want to keep what makes us comfortable close, and what makes us uncomfortable as far away as possible.

But Jesus didn't put up these fences like we do; he tore them down and put up flashing neon welcome signs.

One of the golden rules of missions trips is "Eat what they give you."

There are no picky eaters on a missions trip. For me, struggling to follow this rule was rarely difficult. I love experiencing different cultures through their food. I will say that this rule was easy to follow during the short time I spent serving in Italy. I had very few problems there. Obviously.

I did however become good friends with a Filipino schoolteacher named Kate. She, along with two other friends went to experience a bit of Filipino culture, right there in the heart of Rome.

One of Rome's highest immigrant populations is from the Philippines.

I wanted to experience Kate's culture, as she had been so appreciative in experiencing mine. (A few days prior I cooked eggs, bacon, biscuits and gravy, and pancakes for everyone.) I will admit, sap from a maple tree may sound foreign to a person who has never seen a maple tree, but not as foreign as the eyeballs staring back at me in the meal I was about to eat with Kate! Come to find out, though Filipino food is delicious, it's highly intimidating to dig into. Kate walked us through each step of the process. I enjoyed the experience. I learned something new. I tasted something I never would have tasted before. I got to know Kate a little bit better. I got to expand my horizons.

I love food for that reason. It is a way for people to express their culture to you in a way that also benefits you. It means a lot to share the foods you love with someone else. Food isn't the only place we can identify cultural boundaries and fences that we have put up around ourselves. We can see our fences when talking about T.V. shows, movies, sports, art, music, etc...

When you notice a fence, tear it down.

Jesus made sure he was understanding of everyone he came in contact with. You can see the fences around each disciple when Jesus accepts the invitation to stay in Samaria. Jesus doesn't put up fences. Samaritan, Galilean, Judean? Doesn't matter to Jesus.

We each need to make the decision that we will value people higher than preferences or prejudices.

I stood there with Gabe looking at me like I was going to hate him and his calling. I felt like a fool. I got on his level and apologized from the bottom of my heart for discrediting his calling the day before.

I begged a fifth grader to forgive me.

I learned something that day. It's not worth it to have negative opinions.

It's just not.

Negative opinions aren't worth the damage they cause.

Remember Thumper's rule? "If you don't have anything nice to say, don't say anything at all." The thing you hate could very well be something someone loves.

By hating that thing you insist on hating, you make it impossible to share the Gospel to that person. It's just not worth it.

After that camp season, I became determined to learn how to appreciate soccer. Turns out, soccer is far more complex than I had originally imagined. It requires the team to work together in formation while sprinting and dribbling a ball at the same time. Soccer players are incredible athletes. My friend Felipe played professional soccer in Brazil. Now he coaches college soccer. I sat down with him to learn the sport. I've seen him play. I've heard him strategize. Soccer was far more interesting than I originally thought.

I started going to college soccer games.

I joined the intramural soccer team.

I even started coaching 8th grade soccer!

Sometimes I wear a soccer jersey!

Who am I?

Still me, just being a little more like Jesus.

I know it seems like a big challenge to find something good in the things you don't like. But it's really not.

Am I a soccer fan now? Nope. But I've chose to learn to appreciate it.

God gave people different passions. We should rejoice when we notice a passion different from our own. Who wants to live in a world of just baseball fans? Who wants to live with people who like everything you like?

That's cookie-cutter.

That's boring.

It's no fun at all!

Instead, we get to live in a diverse world with billions of individuals who are all gifted by God with a passion for something.

Every God-given passion is worthy of our admiration and affirmation. We need to learn to rejoice in our diversity. It's what makes us a body.

Sure, I may still favor certain things over others. But I don't need to degrade people when they don't appreciate something like I do.

Jesus was so clearly opposed to prejudice.

Now, when I ask kids what their favorite sport is, I make sure I affirm them. After all, isn't their hard work the goal of sports, anyway?

Are they growing? Are they learning to work as a team? Are they becoming disciplined?

If so, any sport is fine with me, even soccer.

LATE NIGHTS

POOL TABLES

STORMS

BE AVAILABLE TO ENCOURAGE

CHAPTER 14

BE AVAILABLE TO ENCOURAGE

As a pastor, I know that people will need me at inconvenient times.

This means I need to be ready.

The Apostle Paul writes in 2 Timothy 4:2,

"Preach the Word; be ready in season and out of season; reprove, rebuke, and exhort, with complete patience and teaching." [1]

I like how the New Living Translation puts it,

"Preach the Word of God. Be prepared, whether the time is favorable or not. Patiently correct, rebuke, and encourage your people with good teaching." [2]

"Whether the time is favorable or not" is a challenging command.

It requires us to be ready and willing to love even when it's inconvenient.

I take this instruction literally. I decided a while ago to keep my cell phone on at night. I tell people to call if they need anything. They rarely do...

But occasionally, I'll wake up to a phone call in the middle of the night. The person on the other end of that call becomes the most important person in the world to me.

I have a pool table in my basement. And when I take these calls, I'll go downstairs, put them on speaker-phone and play while I listen. As I mentioned in Chapter One, doing something with my hands helps me focus better.

I've had a few friends hang up the phone and come over late at night to play with me.

I like that too.

These phone calls are important. If someone has come to the point where they feel the need to pick up the phone and wake someone up at 2:00 am to talk, I've got to assume it is pretty important.

Most of the time, people just need to hear their own words come out of their mouth.

Sometimes people just need to be affirmed.

Sometimes their perspective is wrong, and they need to be lovingly corrected.

They can always use prayer!

I feel like Jesus in these moments. I'm reminded of the story recorded in Matthew 8, Mark 4, and Luke 8.

Jesus had just finished teaching the crowds and was getting tired. (Ministry has that effect on people.) Jesus told his disciples to get in the boats so they could travel to the other side of the Sea of Galilee. The disciples agreed and cast off the docks for the other side. Depending on where they were on the sea, the trip could've been anywhere from eight to thirteen miles long, plenty of time to take a nap in the boat. A big storm rose up and began to thrash the boats around in the water.

The disciples were terrified; they thought they were going to drown.

Where is Jesus in all this?

Sleeping.

FAITH IS BELIEVING WHAT GOD SAID BEFORE RECEIVING WHAT GOD SAID.

The disciples definitely thought Jesus was crazy for not being scared. After all, who could sleep in a sinking ship?

Do you have a friend like that? Nothing seems to intimidate them? Nothing hurts them. Nothing scares them. They are just unfazed by everything. It kind of makes you wonder if everything is all right in their head. The disciples are looking at Jesus with the same mix of amazement and confusion.

Maybe he has a screw loose or something...

How could anyone sleep through something like this?

They were shocked he wasn't awake, and he is the only person they think can help, so they woke him up.

"Jesus!" They shouted. "Are you serious? You're sleeping? We are about to die! Don't you care that we might drown?"

Jesus sat up from his slumped position and said, "Peace. Be still."

And just like that, as his gentle voice bounced over the waters, one by one each wave settled.

The waters stilled.

The winds calmed.

The boat rested from it's tossing.

"Why are you so fearful?" Jesus asked, "Where is your faith?"

This story is pretty well known. Chances are if you've heard a handful of sermons in your lifetime, you've heard this story. Usually the story serves to remind us that though we may be experiencing storms in our life, we can rely on Jesus.

Jesus is never intimidated by our problems. Jesus is always willing to step in and bring peace to our situations. All we need to do is ask. We need not to worry and have faith that he will keep us safe. Those are great lessons, and totally true.

But this book isn't titled, Be Like The Disciples.

It's titled, Be Like Jesus.

Which begs the question...

What can we learn from Jesus?

Well, for one...

Sometimes other people's storms can affect your beauty sleep.

Their problems might wake you up. You may be exhausted, but some-one could need you. And if they do, just remember that Jesus would wake up.

It's easy to say we need to rest in the name of self-care. There is truth in that. Jesus took naps. Jesus rested. But Jesus was always ready to be interrupted.

When your gas tank is filled up in prayer, a detour isn't a problem.

Secondly, notice how Jesus responds. He doesn't make the disciples feel like they inconvenienced him.

I guarantee, if people think they are an inconvenience to you, they will never ask you for help.

People need someone like Jesus who they can always ask for help without fear of rejection or judgment. Jesus didn't begrudgingly calm the storm. He wasn't grumpy. He wasn't angry. He simply told the storm to be still and then reminded the disciples they have no reason to worry. God cares about them. They need to remember that fact.

Faith believes God is who he says he is.

God said he is our Comforter, our Peace, our Defender, our Savior, our Foundation, our Victory, and much more!

Faith is believing what God said before receiving what God said.

Jesus didn't rebuke the disciples; he rebuked the storm.

It's easy to get mad at people when they inconvenience you.

In this story, however, Jesus was lovingly gracious with the disciples.

I feel like we read Jesus' statement "ye of little faith" as an insult. Or like he's disappointed. Maybe that's because that is how we've been spoken to before. Or maybe that's how we speak to ourselves. When reading scripture, we need to make sure the words we read are consistent with the character of Jesus rather than reading our own emotions into the story.

Jesus isn't disappointed.

Jesus is lovingly revealing to the disciples their lack of something they need.

He is instructing them to be courageous and believe God.

That's not mean spirited.

That's not an insult.

That's not a slight at all.

It's an open invitation to revelation.

Lastly, Jesus doesn't just calm the physical storm on the sea.

He calms the storm of fear in the disciple's hearts.

He says, "Peace. Be still."

A wonderful translation of this statement reads,

"Hush. Be reduced to silence."

The Greek word for "hush" or "peace" is siōpaō. It means an involuntary stillness, silence, or my favorite, a metaphor for a calm sea. I love the emphasis on the word *involuntary*. It's like Jesus is saying, when I show up, you have no choice but to have peace.

The word used for "be still" is phimoō. This word means to be muzzled, or kept in check, or my favorite, *to stop the mouth*.

Sometimes I think when Jesus says "Peace. Be still." He is not only talking to the wind and the waves, but to the disciple's hearts.

The word for peace is sometimes used as a metaphor for a calm sea. Could Jesus have calmed the sea, and then turned to the disciples and said, "Be like the sea. Be stilled." Would they have internalized these words? Seeing the seas calm, the disciples would have learned. If Jesus could influence the physical, how much more could he influence the spiritual?

If Jesus can calm even the most aggressive storm, how much more could he calm our hearts?

Jesus didn't just calm the storm, he calmed the ones who woke him up and asked for help.

When we live like Jesus, we have access to the same peace Jesus accessed to calm the storm and to calm the disciples.

Notice the order of Jesus' role.

He first spoke to the storm.

He then spoke to the disciples.

When we only address the person, we are only dealing with half the problem.

Think of it this way. If you have a child who is running with the wrong crowd and is getting into trouble, a simple encouragement not to participate in the misbehavior will not do the trick. You need to address the friends. You need to remove the influence of the negative friends in your child's life. The enemy makes loud noises. Sometimes those noises are so loud, it becomes hard to hear anything else.

First, we speak to storms.

We have the authority to speak to these situations that hurt people and say, "Be muzzled!" What influences are we allowing to continue speaking when we simply address the person? Yes, they need you to speak into their life.

But it's hard to hear in the middle of a raging storm.

After we silence the storm, we can speak to the person and encourage them to have faith in God. I've seen it time and time again in my own life and the lives of others.

The second part of the process is so beautiful.

You watch people breathe again. That first breath of fresh air after the storm is so beautiful. You can see the demeanor of a person change. You feel the peace of God fill the air. It is such a privilege to participate in this miracle.

In order to participate in this process of peace, it is important to remember a glaringly obvious pre-requisite.

You must be available.

In this story, Jesus wasn't in another boat. He was in the same boat as his disciples. Jesus is present with us in our storms. He isn't outside our storm looking in. He is inside our storm looking out. He sits with us in the midst of the wind and rain and brings a comfort we could not attain apart from his presence.

———

My grandparents have a cottage on a small lake in Michigan.

We spend the summers up there. One of my favorite things to do is sit on the front porch and watch thunderstorms roll across the lake.

The sky turns blackish green, and the lake gets eerily calm. Soon, the super-cell breaks the silence. The waters toss and the far side of the lake becomes eclipsed by rain and lightning. Bolts of lightning fill the sky and the thunder shakes the trees.

There's a reason I like it; other than because I'm a Midwestern boy.

I like watching storms because when I was a kid, I wouldn't sit on the porch alone. I would sit on the porch with my grandpa. I knew he was right there. I knew I was safe. Because he was next to me and I trusted that he would never let anything bad happen to me. I would watch my grandpa laugh at the thunder and smile at the lightning. He was appreciating the unrestrained power of nature. I learned to be calm in storms because my grandpa's response taught me not to be afraid.

In Matthew 14 we see a story unfold, similar to the first story about the storm.

"Immediately he made the disciples get into the boat and go before him to the other side, while he dismissed the crowds. And after he had dismissed the crowds, he went up on the mountain by himself to pray. When evening came, he was there alone, but the boat by this time was a long way from the land, beaten by the waves, for the wind was against them. And in the fourth watch of the night he came to them, walking on the sea. But when the disciples saw him walking on the sea, they were terrified, and said, "It is a ghost!" and they cried out in fear. But immediately Jesus spoke to them, saying, "Take heart; it is I. Do not be afraid. And Peter answered him, "Lord, if it is you, command me to come to

you on the water." He said, "Come." So Peter got out of the boat and walked on the water and came to Jesus. But when he saw the wind, he was afraid, and beginning to sink he cried out, "Lord, save me." Jesus immediately reached out his hand and took hold of him, saying to him, "O you of little faith, why did you doubt?" And when they got into the boat, the wind ceased. And those in the boat worshiped him, saying, "Truly you are the Son of God." [3]

Matthew 14:22-33 ESV

In this story the disciples are in the boat alone, being pounded by the relentless waves and winds. They are freaking out again! To make matters worse, they see a ghost coming to reap their souls! This night is not going well for the disciples. I imagine them telling one another how badly they wish Jesus was with them to calm the storm again.

Then Jesus shows up.

Jesus speaks to the fear they are experiencing. Jesus addresses their lack of faith once more.

> WE CAN'T JUST TALK THE TALK. WE NEED TO WALK THE WALK; EVEN IF IT MEANS WALKING ON WATER.

You may feel like you're in a storm, and God has abandoned you. You may feel like God is far away. But be encouraged, Jesus will bend the laws of physics to make sure you are taken care of. He will come walking on the waves.

In the first story, Jesus sleeps in the boat and then calms the sea.

In the second story, Jesus takes it one step further; literally. He doesn't just calm the storm again. This time, he shows the disciples, if they have faith, they can walk through the storm.

The first story, Jesus sits with the disciples and teaches them the storm isn't something to be feared.

In the second story, Jesus teaches them the storm is something to be conquered.

When we encourage people, it's not enough to simply give lip service to a problem and solution.

Jesus doesn't just calm storms, he walks on them.

When people see us walk on the waves in our own lives and practice what we preach, they are encouraged in a far more practical way than mere words can express. We can't just talk the talk. We need to walk the walk; even if it means walking on water. People need to see you live out your faith in your own life. When we practice what we preach, our sermons gain legitimacy. The people we encourage can see the hope we carry. They can trust the same God who delivered us, will deliver them.

I've never walked on water, but I have gone swimming in a storm. Sometimes, at the lake, we would go swimming when the rain came. (Don't worry, we'd get out of the water if there was lightning). My older cousins would take me out in the water as it began to rain. There is something really fun about swimming in a storm. If you go underwater and look up, you can see the rain fall on the surface. The cold rain makes the water feel like a bath. It's a unique experience to swim in a storm.

I don't fear storms.

I've experienced many storms; both physical and spiritual.

I know that when it comes to encouraging people, sometimes the greatest encouragement isn't found in words alone. I know that people are watching me as I walk through my storms. I don't want to teach the wrong lesson by the way I walk. I want to walk by faith on top of the waves, just like Jesus. And as I master the waves, I will encourage others to step out in faith with me.

I like getting calls late at night.

I like staying up late talking about Jesus.

I like speaking into people's lives and saying, "Peace. Be still."

I like that people are watching me as I walk through my own storms.

I want to be like my grandpa, who sat with me and taught me how to smile during storms.

I want to be like my cousins who taught me to swim in the rain.

I want to be like Jesus, who was always available to encourage his friends.

Jesus was present in the storms. Both times. The second time, he made a little more of a dramatic entrance. He was still there. All it took was for the disciples to call on him.

And he answered.

And he will always answer.

Every time.

Even late at night.

JULY 4TH FIREWORKS THE GOSPEL

LIVE OUT THE GOSPEL

CHAPTER 15

LIVE OUT THE GOSPEL

The Fourth of July is my favorite holiday.

Yeah, Christmas is the most wonderful time of the year, but for me the best day of the year is Independence Day.

I even have a pair of swim trunks that turn into an American flag when you get them wet.

I love the Fourth of July. It is the height of summer, the crux of the vacationing season. School is out and fun is in! For my family and me, that means it is time to go to the lake.

Our cottage sits within a community of cottages called Island Park Recreation Club. IPRC is smack dab in the middle of two lakes. We have tennis courts; a basketball court, a softball diamond, and antique playground equipment that are still the highlights of the park. It's the perfect little sumer neighborhood.

Each July 4th, there is a display of fireworks over one of the lakes.

Before the firework show, the park has tons of activities.

We play bingo.

We have a cakewalk.

There is a talent show for the kids.

Some years, we have a chicken roast that fills up the entire street.

But all of those festivities are just precursors to the fireworks.

People come from all over the area to see our fireworks. The docks and shores are covered in picnic blankets and folding chairs. If you have a boat, it's in the water, cast off the dock so you can get a closer seat.

Year after year, the crowd of people fills this little summer town in southern Michigan.

We sit down at dusk and get ready for the show.

At the first explosion of fireworks all eyes are turned toward the sky. Colors and sparkles fill the air. The powerful explosions rattle your chest as you smell the smoke carried by the breeze from the other side of the lake. During the firework show everyone is a kid again. We all watch the sky in amazement. It's a clear, cool, summer night. I sit on the shore of a lake with my friends and family and we watch the fireworks.

After about fifteen minutes the fireworks die down. Just a few are shot off at a time. They seem to be over.

Every year, we watch and wait.

Is the show over?

Should we pack up and go home?

But year after year we know in the back of our minds we haven't yet seen the grand finale.

Suddenly, the sky lights up again. The rhythm of the first part of the show is over. There is no rhyme or reason for the colors or shapes of the fireworks now. The grand finale looks like they set all the fireworks off at once. People cheer and clap as the barrage of what sounds like cannon fire deafens the masses. Though it is dark, the extravagance of the sky on fire makes it possible to see the smiles on every face. After the grand finale, a cheer erupts from the lake as loud as the finale itself. It is at this point each year when we walk back to the cottage.

When we get home, we go out on the front deck facing the lake and get out the sparklers.

You remember sparklers, right?

Fire on a stick made for kids to run around with.

> **THE GOSPEL IS NOT A TICKET TO HEAVEN. THE GOSPEL IS A SPARKLER IN YOUR HAND.**

What could possibly go wrong?

All the kids will run around enjoying these miniature portable firework shows. When I was a kid, we would light multiple sparklers in each hand and run around the yard. Who am I kidding, I still do this! We'd wave the flaming batons around in shapes and letters, trying to spell our names in the air. Once the sparklers were gone, we would sit around the bonfire and tell stories until it was time to close our eyes and let the sound of distant firecrackers sing us to sleep. It is a perfect day full of fun, friends, family, and pyrotechnic displays of patriotism.

I love the Fourth of July.

I think it has to do with the nostalgia of it all. However, I have noticed that perhaps another reason I love the Fourth of July is because it shares the same cadence of the Gospel.

It is called Independence Day after all...

The entire day, people are enjoying the holiday, all while waiting for one thing. We are expecting the firework show. We are waiting for the light to be revealed in the darkness. Just like the people of God were waiting for their Messiah. The whole earth was waiting for Jesus to come. The captives of sin were anticipating the glory and power of God to be revealed to them.

Then the fireworks begin. [1]

The fireworks are the ministry of Jesus. Both the beauty and power of God were on full display for the three years Jesus was ministering. All eyes were on Jesus. All eyes were on the kingdom of Heaven, as it manifested on Earth. The show lasted a while. People loved what they were seeing. Jesus was drawing a crowd.

Just like that, the fireworks stopped. [2]

Jesus was arrested, crucified, and buried in a tomb. The sky grew dark again. The light of the world was gone.

The glory and beauty of God ceased to be on public display.

Nobody could believe it.

Some gave up hope that the sky would ever light up again.

Jesus was dead.

They packed up their blankets and chairs. The suspense grew. The hope began to dim, until the fuse was lit for the grand finale. [3]

Suddenly, out of the stillness of the night, an explosion of glory unlike anything humanity had ever witnessed. The sheer power of the resurrection was shaking the ground. It was pounding on our hearts. A roar of angels rejoiced as the Son of God had overcome the darkness and put on full display the glory of God! [4]

Following the dramatic conclusion of the firework show that is Jesus' life, he sent us back home to our individual communities and families. But he didn't send us back empty-handed, he gave us his Spirit.

Finally, with Holy Spirit sparklers in hand, the masses disbanded into the earth carrying the same glory and beauty of Jesus with them. [5]

"Here's another way to put it: You're here to be light, bringing out the God-colors in the world. God is not a secret to be kept. We're going public with this, as public as a city on a hill. If I make you light-bearers, you don't think I'm going to hide you under a bucket, do you? I'm putting you on a light stand. Now that I've put you there on a hilltop, on a light stand—shine! Keep open house; be generous with your lives. By opening up to others, you'll prompt people to open up with God, this generous Father in Heaven." [6]

Matthew 5:14-16 MSG

What is the Gospel?

Simple. Jesus established us in the right position, took away every hindrance, and empowered us to live like him.

We do not receive this gift of radical grace for ourselves.

The Gospel is not a ticket to Heaven. The Gospel is a sparkler in your hand. The Gospel is an invitation for all of us to join in on the great task to light up the world with God's glory.

So be proud of your light, because it is a gift from your God.

Be present with those around you.

Live like you're winning.

Look for tiny pieces of paper.

Share the story of God.

Be patient in the desert.

Focus on following.

Sacrifice for love.

Know how to goof around.

Practice reciprocal submission.

Protect your purpose.

Do good, whatever, wherever.

Stay filled up in prayer.

Put up welcome signs, not fences.

Be available to encourage.

Live out the Gospel.

Be like Jesus.

BE
LIKE
JESUS

CONCLUSION

As we come to the end of this book, I would like to bring your attention all the way back to the front cover. If you haven't already, I want you to go ahead and tear off the corner of the cover down the dotted line.

In our effort to be like Jesus, there is one final consideration I want to ask you to remember.

Being like Jesus is not an achievement.

It's not an accomplishment.

It's not a destination.

Being like Jesus is a process...

This process requires us to remember, as long as we live we will be moving toward the likeness of Christ, yet never attaining that goal in full here in our lifetime.

Because of this reality, Paul instructs the Philippians to put no confidence in their flesh.

"Finally, my brothers, rejoice in the Lord. To write the same things to you is no trouble to me and is safe for you. Look out for the dogs, look out for the evildoers, look out for those who mutilate the flesh. For we are the circumcision, who worship by the Spirit of God and glory in Christ Jesus and put no confidence in the flesh—though I myself have reason for confidence in the

flesh also. If anyone else thinks he has reason for confidence in the flesh, I have more: circumcised on the eighth day, of the people of Israel, of the tribe of Benjamin, a Hebrew of Hebrews; as to the law, a Pharisee; as to zeal, a persecutor of the church; as to righteousness under the law, blameless. But whatever gain I had, I counted as loss for the sake of Christ. Indeed, I count everything as loss because of the surpassing worth of knowing Christ Jesus my Lord. For his sake I have suffered the loss of all things and count them as rubbish, in order that I may gain Christ and be found in him, not having a righteousness of my own that comes from the law, but that which comes through faith in Christ, the righteousness from God that depends on faith— that I may know him and the power of his resurrection, and may share his sufferings, becoming like him in his death, that by any means possible I may attain the resurrection from the dead." [1]

Philippians 3:1-11 ESV

Paul is telling the church to remember our salvation is not about our behavior, it's about Jesus. We need to remember even the best of us are broken people in need of grace. We **"fall short of the glory of God"** [2] every single day!

A good way to paraphrase that is "We do things that Jesus wouldn't do."

Paul continues on with one of my favorite statements in verse twelve, **"Not that I have already obtained this or am already perfect, but I press on to make it my own, because Christ Jesus has made me his own."** [3]

Paul says, "Listen guys, I'm not perfect either. We are all trying to be like Jesus every day, more and more, little by little." Then he closes the thought by saying, "Just keep trying; the best you can... day by day. Keep Jesus as your example for how to live life. Remember that he loves you and chose you and wants to make you like him!"

This exhortation is so encouraging!

I want to encourage you, just like Paul encouraged the Philippians; it's about the process. It's about the race. It's about the growth.

Have you ever heard the saying, "You can't judge a book by its cover"?

Everyone seems to say that, but few seem to listen.

It seems like everywhere we go, people are judging us by "our cover". It feels like people are always watching us, ready to pounce the moment we show any weakness. It's easy to feel the pressure to make sure our cover is perfect.

But when we refuse to be transparent about our weaknesses, we deceive those around us. We make it look like we have it all together. We make it look like we are not broken and flawed. For some reason, acting perfect makes us feel like we are representing Jesus well. On the contrary!

When we act like we have it all together, we deny Jesus the ability to make his grace known through us.

In 2 Corinthians 12:9 Paul says, **"But he said to me, "My grace is sufficient for you, for my power is made perfect in weakness." Therefore I will boast all the more gladly of my weaknesses, so that the power of Christ may rest upon me."** [4]

When we don't try and cover up our torn and imperfect cover, we actually reveal Jesus.

When we share how our natural proclivities are toward things contrary to the way of Jesus, yet, we practice the way of Jesus - people see the work of the Holy Spirit in us! Had they not known we were quick to become angry, God would not get glory when they see our patience. If our neighbors were unaware of our selfish desires, when we give freely and generously to others, God would not get the glory.

> Were clay to throw itself upon the wheel
> and freely form a vessel of use.
> No potter near could dare to steal
> the honor which the clay is due.

That is to say, when we neglect to share our weakness, we take credit for our good behavior. When we show our weakness, and walk in strength, it is no doubt that the Lord is the one responsible. We can't act like we are perfect, we are being perfected by a brilliant potter.

So, we live authentic lives, sharing our struggles with one another and being open about our journey.

We make it known that Jesus is the well of grace we continually draw from.

We embrace the process and keep our eyes set on Jesus.

Because one day, when we meet the Lord face to face, we will behold his glory.

His goodness.

His beauty.

As we stare into the glory of Jesus, we will be completely transformed into his likeness. We will finally, 100%, totally, completely, be like Jesus!

Until then, remember to embrace the process. Don't be discouraged by your shortfalls. Romans 8:1 says, **"There is therefore now no condemnation for those who are in Christ Jesus."** [5]

We can have confidence in Jesus.

Trust his glorious grace!

Believe his wonderful mercy!

And embrace his generous love!

I have one final thought to share before I let you put the book down.

My friend encouraged me to write out declarative statements to speak over myself each morning. These statements are simple truths I want to make sure I never forget. Among them are: *God knows me personally. Life is a gift. Creativity is in my DNA.* But perhaps my favorite of them all is:

I live like Jesus more often than not.

It's easy to get caught up in our deficiencies. It's good to understand and be open about our weaknesses. But dwelling on all those shortcomings is never going to benefit us. We are always growing more like Christ. That's the goal right? I fail. I'm not perfect. But every day, I make more choices to be like Jesus than I make choices to not be like Jesus. I want to remind myself that I'm winning this fight against my flesh. It's not by my own ability, but by Jesus' strength that I am winnning. My focus is on Jesus. I boast in my weakness. But I also acknowledge that I'm doing a good job.

And so are you.

Keep being like Jesus.

May the Lord bless you
and protect you.
May the Lord smile on you
and be gracious to you.
May the Lord show you his favor
and give you his peace. [6]

Amen

NOTES

INTRODUCTION
1. Ephesians 5:1 ESV

CHAPTER 1
1. 2 Corinthians 13:15 ESV
2. John 11:17-27 ESV

CHAPTER 2
1. John 16:7 ESV
2. 1 Timothy 2:4 ESV
3. Acts 1:8 ESV
4. Acts 11:26 ESV
5. Luke 4:18 ESV
6. Peterson, Jordan B. 12 Rules For Life: An Antidote To Chaos. Random House Canada, 2018.
7. Solzhenitsyn, Aleksandr. The Gulag Archipelago. The Harvill Press London, 1986
8. In Christ Alone, Keith Getty, Stuart Townend, 2001
9. Psalm 118:6 ESV
10. Luke 23:34 ESV
11. Romans 8:11 ESV
12. Romans 8:35-39 ESV

CHAPTER 3
1. Colossians 3:23-24 ESV
2. Colossians 3:23-24 MSG
3. John 5:2-9 ESV

CHAPTER 4

1. Matthew 13:1-9 ESV
2. Matthew 13:11-16 ESV
3. Luke 9:57-62 ESV
4. Gallo, Carmine. Talk Like TED. Pan Books Ltd, 2016.

CHAPTER 5

1. Matthew 4:1 ESV
2. Luke 4:14 ESV
3. See also: Lou Engle Digging the Wells of Revival: Reclaiming Your Historic Inheritance Through Prophetic Intercession
4. Romans 5:3-4 ESV
5. Galatians 1:11-17 ESV
6. Psalm 63:1 ESV

CHAPTER 6

1. Maxwell, John C. Becoming a Person of Influence: How to Positively Impact the Lives of Others, HarperCollins Leadership, 1997.
2. Matthew 8:1-4 ESV
3. Proverbs 4:10-15 ESV
4. Matthew 18:6 ESV
5. Proverbs 4:18-19 ESV
6. Matthew 9:27-31 ESV
7. Mark 8:22-26 ESV
8. John 9:1-7 ESV

CHAPTER 7

1. See also: The Wisdom of the Desert Fathers and Mothers,

Paraclete Press, 2010.

2. Romans 16:15-17 ESV

3. Philippians 2:5-8 MSG

4. James 4:7 ESV

5. Chan, Francis. Letters to The Church, David C. Cook, 2019.

6. Boyd, Greg. The Myth of a Christian Religion: Losing Your Religion for the Beauty of a Revolution, Zondervan, 2009

INTERMISSION

1. Willard, Dallas. The Spirit of the Disciplines: Understanding How God Changes Lives, HarperOne, Reprint edition 1999.

CHAPTER 8

1. Proverbs 29:23 ESV

2. Noce Ball is a cross between dodgeball, baseball, and ultimate frisbee. It has become a favorite Opportunity Cell at Hot Rock over the years. It is a chaotic and ever-changing game that develops adaptability and teamwork. Super fun! Yes, it is named Noce Ball after my dad, the game's inventor.

3. Mark 10:42-45 ESV

4. Mark 10:41-45 MSG

5. John 13:12-17 ESV

CHAPTER 9

1. John 2:6-11 ESV

2. Philippians 2:3-4 ESV

3. Psalms 133:1 ESV

4. Ephesians 5:15-21 ESV

5. rfk.org

6. Luke 8:43-48

7. John 5:1-15

8. Mark 10-46-52
9. Luke 19-1-10
10. Matthew 8:5-13
11. Matthew 15:22-29
12. Luke 4:18-19 ESV

CHAPTER 10
1. Luke 2:41-51 ESV
2. Luke 1:26-33 ESV
3. Matthew 1:19-23 ESV
4. Leviticus 19:2 ESV
5. 1 Corinthians 7:7-9 ESV
6. 1 Corinthians 7:17 ESV
7. 1 Corinthians 7:32-35 ESV
8. Philippians 3:14 ESV
9. Isaiah 50:7 ESV

CHAPTER 11
1. Fred Rogers, Mister Rogers' Neighborhood, Competition: A Favorite Factory Visit, Crayons!, PBS, 1981.
2. Romans 11:36 ESV
3. Genesis 1:1-3 ESV
4. John 1:1-5 ESV
5. Matthew 15:21-28 ESV

CHAPTER 12
1. Luke 5:16 ESV
2. Mark 1:35 ESV
3. Matthew 14:23 ESV
4. Matthew 21:22 ESV

CHAPTER 13

1. John 4:39-45 ESV
2. 1 Corinthians 9:19-23 ESV

CHAPTER 14

1. 2 Timothy 4:2 ESV
2. 2 Timothy 4:2 NLT
3. Matthew 14:22-33 ESV

CHAPTER 15

1. Isaiah 52-53
2. John 1:14, John 6:38, John 14:10, Hebrews 1:3
3. Matthew 27:59-60, Mark 15:33, 1 Corinthians 2:8
4. Revelation 1:17-18, 1 Corinthians 15:20, Luke 24:1-8
5. Acts 1:8, Matthew 28:18-20
6. Matthew 5:14-16 MSG

CONCLUSION

1. Philippians 3:1-11 ESV
2. Romans 3:23 ESV
3. Philippians 3:12 ESV
4. 2 Corinthians 12:9 ESV
5. Romans 8:1 ESV
6. Numbers 6:24-26 NLT

Stay Connected with
BE LIKE JESUS

@BeLikeJesusBook

BeLikeJesusBook.com

church
is a
circle

circle
BOX

Creative group curriculum
to engage and empower you
to share and grow in the story
of God within community.

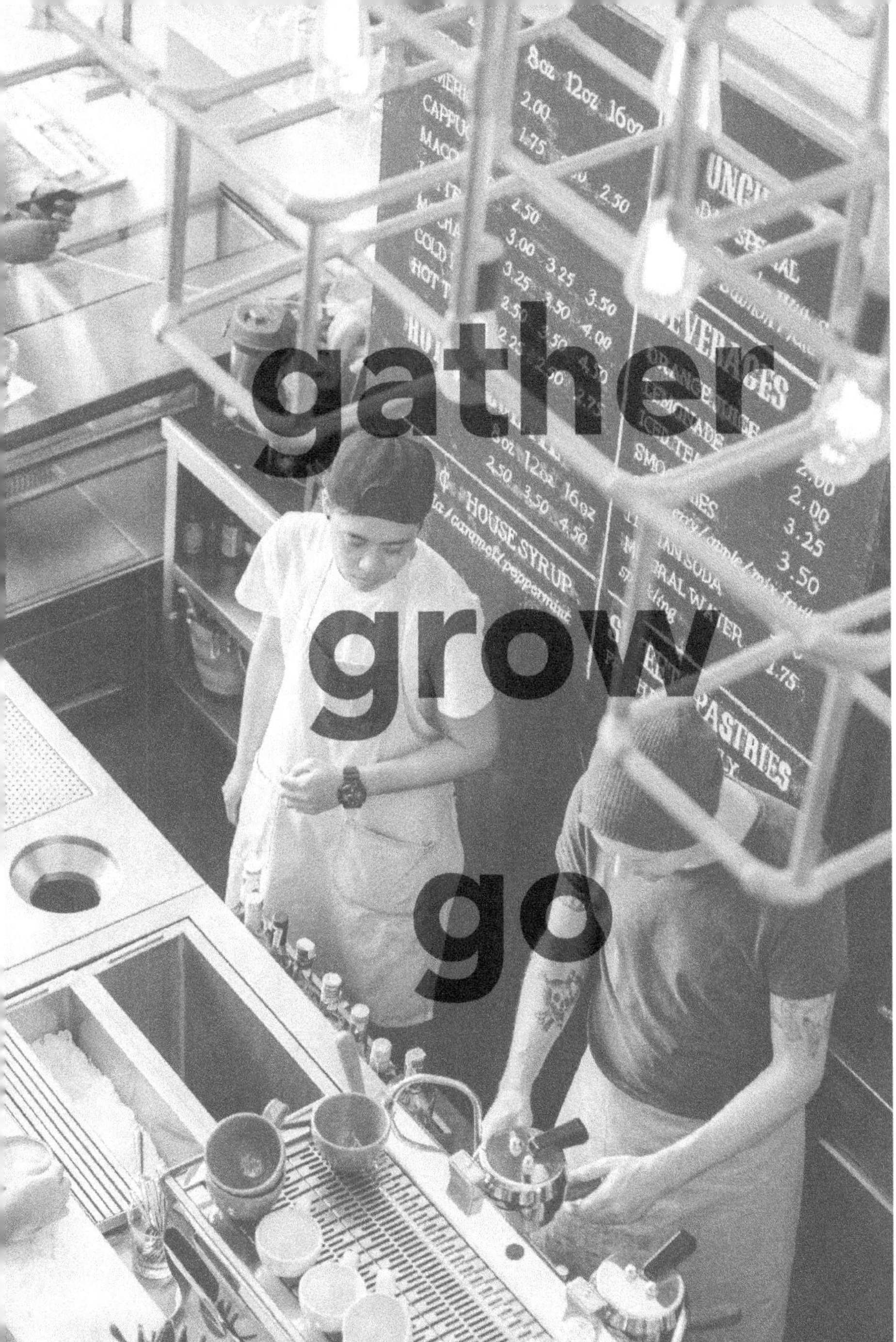
gather
grow
go
8oz 12oz 16oz
HOUSE SYRUP
PASTRIES

CPSIA information can be obtained
at www.ICGtesting.com
Printed in the USA
FSHW021455271020